The financing procedures of British foreign trade

The financing procedures of British foreign trade

STEPHEN CARSE
JOHN WILLIAMSON
GEOFFREY E. WOOD

CAMBRIDGE UNIVERSITY PRESS
CAMBRIDGE
LONDON · NEW YORK · NEW ROCHELLE
MELBOURNE · SYDNEY

Published by the Press Syndicate of the University of Cambridge
The Pitt Building, Trumpington Street, Cambridge CB2 1RP
32 East 57th Street, New York, NY 10022, USA
296 Beaconsfield Parade, Middle Park, Melbourne 3206, Australia

First published 1980.

Photoset and printed in Malta
by Interprint Limited

Library of Congress Cataloguing in Publication Data
Carse, Stephen.
The financing procedures of British foreign trade.
Bibliography: p.
Includes index.
1. Foreign exchange problem – Great Britain.
I. Williamson, John, 1937– joint author.
II. Wood, Geoffrey Edward, joint author. III. Title.
HG3943.C37 382.1′7′0941 79-18146
ISBN 0 521 22534 5

To the memory of our colleague and friend Fred Hirsch

CONTENTS

TABLES

PREFACE

The research project whose results are presented in this book originated from a suggestion of Fred Hirsch, who was at that time a colleague of two of the present authors at the University of Warwick. The three of us accordingly formulated a research proposal which we submitted to the Ford Foundation's programme for research into the International Economic Order. We received approval from the Ford Foundation in the summer of 1975, and in October of that year the third of the present authors, Stephen Carse, commenced employment on the project. Before the first set of questionnaires was despatched, Fred Hirsch had contracted a progressive and irreversible muscular illness, of which he died some 20 months later while drafting of the monograph was in progress. He was in no position to do any of the drafting himself and saw very little of the final manuscript. Since authorship implies responsibility for what is written, we therefore cannot claim him as a joint author. Instead, we take this opportunity of acknowledging his role in inspiring and guiding the study and of paying tribute to the dedication which he showed to the end in keeping us up to the mark. Rarely can it have been more apt to express thanks for help while giving absolution for errors or inadequacies.

Four other expressions of thanks are in order. First, to the Ford Foundation, not just for their provision of financial support which made the project possible, but for their flexibility in extending the duration of the grant, thus permitting successful conclusion of the project despite problems which no doubt included planning deficiences on our part. Second, to the almost 2,000 firms that took the trouble of filling out our questionnaire. We are well aware that completing questionnaires has a real resource cost, but we hope that those who helped us will judge the effort to have been worth while in view of the results presented in the following pages. Third, to Iain Liddell for his work in programming the computer to assemble and analyse our results. Finally, to Mrs Joy

Gardner for her secretarial support during the project and her usual efficient typing of the manuscript.

Stephen Carse
John Williamson
Geoffrey E. Wood

INTRODUCTION

The study reported in this monograph was centred on an attempt to discover the financing practices currently prevalent in British foreign trade. By 'financing practices' we mean the arrangements made for collecting or making payments for exports or imports – the currency in which the invoice is drawn up, whether the transaction is covered in the forward market, the method of settlement adopted, and what is implied for the length and elasticity of the period of credit. Systematic investigation of this subject is relatively new, having been pioneered by Sven Grassman in Sweden in the late 1960s. We have aimed to discover comparable data for the UK, and we report these data in this monograph in the context of an attempt to advance understanding of the reasons for, and the consequences of, existing practices.

1 Purposes of the study

The financing practices used in foreign trade are important from both microeconomic and macroeconomic viewpoints.

The microeconomic standpoint is that of the individual firm engaged in trade. The financial terms (other than price) offered by an exporting firm constitute one aspect of its overall competitiveness. An appropriate choice of those financial terms may make it possible for an exporter or importer to improve its own prospective return, or decrease its exposure to risk, without a commensurate cost to its trading partner. Under certain circumstances this may, for example, be accomplished by covering in the forward market; and at times it has also been claimed, perhaps somewhat simplistically, that it can be accomplished by invoicing exports in strong foreign currencies rather than weak sterling. In any event, one reason for regarding the topic as significant is that the practices adopted, and the constraints on those practices imposed by official regulations, influence the efficiency with which firms can conduct trade and hence the benefits which they derive from it.

The macroeconomic viewpoint is that of the managers of the economy, the Treasury and the Bank of England. After the 1967 devaluation of sterling there was much discussion of the lagged, and, indeed, initially perverse, response of the balance of payments. Several explanations of this 'J-curve effect' were offered, ranging from the misjudgment of the British government in inadequately reducing home demand, through the assertion that it was attributable to the long delay in devaluation which had allowed productive capacity in the export industries to atrophy, to the claim that a lagged response was inevitable because production and trading patterns are always slow to adjust. This matter has never really been resolved satisfactorily, but what has become increasingly recognised in the intervening years is that a *short-run* J-curve (shorter than that which followed the 1967 devaluation) is quite likely to be the mechanical result of invoicing practices. Suppose, for example, that all British exports are invoiced in sterling and all British imports in foreign exchange. Then the immediate effect of a sterling depreciation on earnings from transactions agreed before the exchange rate change took effect would be to reduce the foreign exchange received from exports while leaving unchanged that needed to pay for imports. Since virtually all trade transactions are agreed some time before payment is due, it follows that under the invoicing practices assumed in this example a depreciation leads to a short-run worsening of the balance of payments, i.e. to a J-curve. The invoicing practices prevalent in the UK do in fact approximate to the pattern postulated above, as we report in Chapter 4. How short the short run is depends on the length of the period of credit, on which we report in Chapter 5. The implications of this for the stability of the foreign exchange market are analysed in Chapter 6.

A second consequence of trade financing practices with important macroeconomic implications is the scope provided for 'leads and lags'. The term 'leads and lags' refers to variations in the timing of purchases or sales of foreign currencies in connection with payments for goods – 'leads' referring to accelerated purchases for payments for imports, and 'lags' to delayed sales of the receipts from payments for exports.[1] Both enable traders to engage in the export of short-term capital. In fact, leading and lagging – shifts in the timing of payments for commercial transactions – at the time the data for this study were gathered provided the only way in which UK residents could move funds abroad legally, on a net basis, without obtaining explicit exchange control permission. The significance of this limitation in exchange control coverage has long been recognised, most notably in the writings of Paul Einzig. But there has been very little attempt to quantify the capital movements that could be effected through leading and lagging. We attempt such a quantification, on the basis of our empirical enquiry into credit terms and methods of settlement, in Chapter 6.

2 Outline of the book

Chapter 1 lays the foundations. We describe in some detail what is involved in the financing of a trade transaction, paying particular attention to the time sequence involved. Using Ronald McKinnon's recent work, we then analyse what behaviour microeconomic theory would lead one to expect to observe. We derive eight testable hypotheses, some of which are strikingly at variance with a traditional view known as the 'vehicle currency hypothesis'.

Chapter 2 provides a summary of the existing body of knowledge on the topics within the scope of our study.

In Chapter 3 we describe the methods by which our data were collected. This chapter includes the questionnaires we sent out, and explains the purposes of the questions that we asked. It also includes the results of some interviews with bankers who were engaged in trade financing, and of another set of interviews with a few of the firms who responded to our questionnaire.

Chapter 4 is devoted to the presentation of our results on the choice of the currency of invoice and the use of the forward market. We first describe our results, and then use them to test six of the eight hypotheses developed in Chapter 1. Chapter 5 contains a parallel account of our results on the choice of the method of settlement and credit terms. These two chapters constitute the core of the book.

In Chapter 6 we discuss the analytical implications of our results, concerning the behaviour of the foreign exchange market. Finally, in Chapter 7, we turn to drawing out such policy implications as our study seems to suggest. We consider policy implications for business, for the management of the UK economy, and for the organisation of the international monetary system.

Postscript

After this book had gone to press, the context of our study was altered by the abolition of UK exchange controls. This means that certain parts of our study are now best viewed as a contribution to economic history. We certainly do not regard this as cause for complaint, particularly as at the end of our book we declare our sympathy for a liberalisation of exchange controls (p. 138).

1

ANALYTICAL FOUNDATIONS

This chapter starts by providing a background description of what is involved in the financing of a foreign trade transaction. The aspects we choose to emphasise are, naturally, those that are of economic significance: the time profile of a trade transaction, the implications of different methods of settlement for the length and flexibility of the period of credit provided by the exporter to the importer, and the exchange control regulations to which the process of trade financing was subject. We then turn to deriving a series of testable hypotheses about the determinants of three of the principal aspects of the financing process. The chapter as a whole provides an introduction to the economics of the financing of foreign trade.

1.1 Background description of trade financing procedures

The time profile of a typical foreign trade transaction is displayed schematically in Figure 1.1. The 'real' events shown in the top portion of the figure normally occur in the sequence shown, although

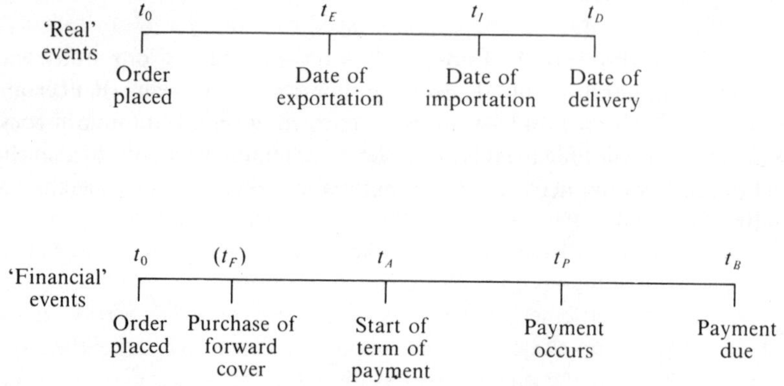

Figure 1.1 The time profile of a foreign trade transaction

even this statement requires qualification: t_D may precede t_I and even t_E, in exceptional cases where the importer takes delivery of the shipment unusually early, before it arrives in his country. The process always starts with an order placed at a time t_0; typically this is also the time at which the contract is signed, although sometimes a number of orders may be placed under a single contract. At some subsequent time t_E the goods are delivered by the exporter to the port and are registered with the Customs of the exporting country. After a delay that may vary from a few minutes in the case of countries with a common frontier to several months where a long sea voyage is involved, the goods are registered by the Customs of the importing country at a time t_I.[1] The importer takes delivery of the goods at a time t_D, typically though by no means invariably after a further brief delay. It may be noted that trade statistics compiled on the customary 'transactions basis' relate to the trade transactions registered by the Customs authorities on the dates t_E and t_I.

The 'financial' events shown in the bottom portion of Figure 1.1 can vary even more than the 'real' events of the top portion. The contract, which is normally signed when the order is placed at t_0, includes provisions governing the financial side of the transaction. These may be divided into (a) specification of the sum that is to be paid, expressed in a particular currency (the 'invoice currency'); and (b) stipulation of a method to determine the date (t_B) on or by which payment should be made. The latter can be subdivided into (i) choice of a 'method of settlement' (also known as a 'form of payment' or 'form of contract'), i.e. of the legal form to be used in acknowledging the financial obligations of the buyer; and (ii) choice of a 'term of payment', which is the period from the time (t_A) when the exporter demands payment by despatching invoice, presenting documents, or requiring acceptance, up to t_B. The contract does not govern the fourth topic which is of interest in this study, namely, whether cover is sought in the forward market; whether to seek such cover is a unilateral decision faced by a party with an exposed foreign exchange position.[2] Presumably a firm taking out forward cover normally does so at a time t_F shortly after the order is placed (we say 'presumably' because this is not a topic on which our survey was designed to shed light). However, there certainly exist circumstances under which t_F might occur later, even after the start of the term of payment t_A – notably if exchange rates, or the firm's expectations thereof, change after t_0 in a way that alters the balance of advantage perceived by the firm between holding an open or a covered position.

Methods of settlement take a wide variety of legal forms. It is convenient to group these into three economic categories, depending on whether they allow the buyer a period of credit and, if so, as to whether or not this period is flexible.

1.1.1 No credit

Under a typical contract of this type, the buyer has to pay for the goods as soon as they are ready for delivery, and cannot take possession until he has done so. In this case t_D, t_A, t_P (the date when payment is actually made and received – we ignore any minor discrepancy between the two) and t_B are coincident, as shown in Figure 1.2 (which reproduces the lower portion of Figure 1.1, with the date of delivery t_D added, for the case of a typical contract of this type).

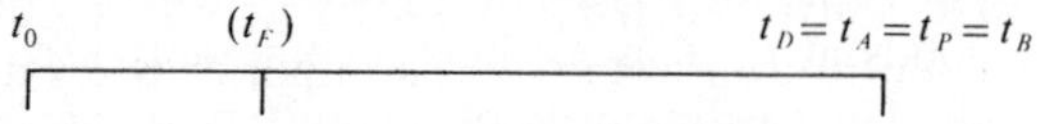

Figure 1.2

The legal forms of contract that fall in this category are cash on delivery, cash against documents, payment of bills against documents, sight documentary credits, and payment in advance. (These terms are defined in Section 3.2, pp. 42–44.) In the latter case, which seems to be very rare in practice, t_B *and* t_P occur before t_D. It is far more common, however, for the buyer to be allowed a few days' grace to check the shipment for quality, which means that t_B and t_P occur slightly after t_D and t_A.

1.1.2 Fixed credit

Contracts involving a fixed period of credit to the buyer fall into two main categories: those which are settled by a single payment, and those which involve a series of instalment payments.

The legal forms of payment with a fixed period of credit and a single payment are the acceptance bill, the term bill, and time documentary credits. Under the first of these, for example, the exporter draws a bill with a fixed term, expressed in the same currency as the invoice, on the importer. This is delivered to the importer at the same time as the goods, which he is allowed to receive only on condition that he 'accepts' the bill; this means that he guarantees to pay the bill's holder when the bill matures. The exporter may then hold this bill or he may sell it, e.g. to his bank, in which case he would receive payment (less some discount) before the buyer pays. The bank rather than the exporter would then be providing the credit to the importer – although the exporter would continue to bear the risk of the importer defaulting (unless he had cover from the Export Credits Guarantee Department, ECGD). In the typical case described above, t_D and t_A are coincident and are followed after a fixed length of time by t_P and t_B, which are also coincident: this typical sequence is illustrated in Figure 1.3. In some cases, however, the start of the term of payment may be measured from the date of invoice or

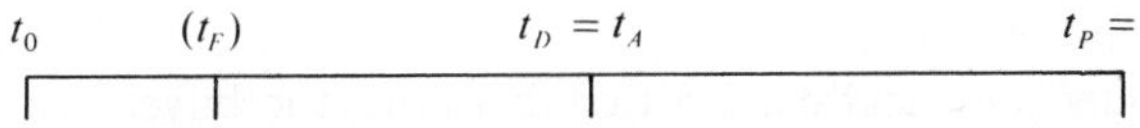

Figure 1.3

despatch of documentation rather than on sight or acceptance of a bill or documentation, in which case t_A would somewhat precede t_D.

Contracts involving instalment payments normally require an advance payment for a portion of the cost prior to despatch of the goods at t_E, followed by a series of payments (often also made with bills) after receipt of the goods at t_D. This method is commonly used for payments for capital goods. The vast majority of 'advance payments' seem to fall in this category, rather than involving advance payment of the whole amount and therefore falling in the 'no-credit' category.

1.1.3 *Variable credit*

The typical example of a contract involving flexibility of the period of credit is the sale on open account. At some date t_A which is normally close to t_E, the seller sends an invoice specifying the date t_B (which will normally fall after t_D) by which payment is due. The buyer is given the freedom to settle within that period, although he may be offered a discount for early or prompt payment. Thus t_P normally precedes t_B, as shown in Figure 1.4. However, due to the lack of formal documentation the seller would find it difficult to invoke legal sanctions against a purchaser who delayed payment for a limited period beyond the due date, so that t_P can in practice follow t_B on occasion. Because of this weakness of the sanctions available against a purchaser who postpones payment, open account is a technique that one would expect to find used only in transactions involving trading partners between whom there is a good deal of trust. On the other hand it is administratively the simplest procedure, so that one would certainly expect to find it employed where the necessary trust exists and there are no countervailing disadvantages.

A procedure sometimes employed when two firms have frequent transactions is for the account to be settled at regular intervals, for example, on the last day of each month. This has usually been treated as a form of open account, although it is not clear that it allows the same degree of flexibility to the importer in choice of the credit term as does the normal version. Another practice sometimes treated as a variant of open account is 'consignment', where an importer agrees to make

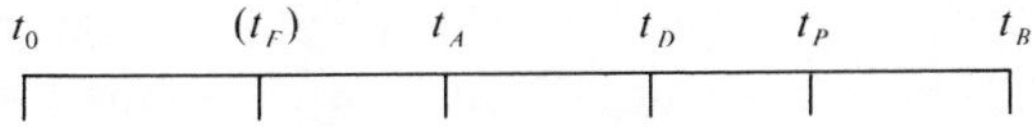

Figure 1.4

payment when, but only when, he has himself sold a shipment. This certainly results in a credit term that is variable from the standpoint of the exporter, but it is not clear that it provides the same scope for leading and lagging as does the typical form of open account.

It is useful at this point to define more precisely what is meant by the 'period of credit', which is in fact a highly ambiguous concept. We shall use the term 'period of credit' generically when the particular concept involved is unimportant, while we have measured it empirically in four ways, on the basis of the following four concepts.

(a) The 'term of payment'. This is the period of time stipulated in the contract for payment, e.g. '30 days on open account', or '60 day bills'. It is the time allowed to the importer *ex ante*, measured from the date t_A when payment is first demanded. In terms of our nomenclature, this concept is represented by $(t_B - t_A)$.

(b) The 'credit term'. This is the *ex post* version of concept *A*. It is the period from the commencement of the term of payment to the date when payment is actually received, or $(t_P - t_A)$.

(c) The 'credit term (revised concept)'. One criticism of concepts *A* and *B* is that they measure the start of the period of credit by an event – the date of invoice, documentation, or acceptance – that is to some extent arbitrary. In particular, the date when the invoice for an open account transaction is despatched is not in itself of any economic significance. Consider an exporter selling goods with a normal transit time of 30 days; whether he sends out invoices at t_E with a 60-day term of payment, or 20 days later with a 40-day term, is inconsequential, but both *A* and *B* concepts would register a longer period of credit in the former case. To correct for this it is natural to replace t_A by t_D, the date of delivery. We have made this change to concept *B* to get *C*, but have not made a similar revision to concept *A*, mainly because the use of concept *A* is traditional. (It would be simple to calculate a similar 'revised concept of the term of payment' by subtracting the excess of *B* over *C* from *A*, should it appear useful.) The revised concept of the credit term is $(t_P - t_D)$.[3]

(d) The 'credit period'. This is Grassman's term (1973a, Chap. 3) for the period that elapses between the time the goods are registered by Customs and the date that payment is made or received. For exports this is $(t_P - t_E)$, and for imports it is $(t_P - t_I)$. One obviously expects that credit periods for exports will tend to exceed those for imports, because of the time $(t_I - t_E)$ taken in transit. One reason for being interested in credit periods is that their variations lead to deviations between the trade balance on a transactions basis and that measured on a payments basis.

In addition to these four concepts of the period of credit, we have measured the time between the order date t_0 and the date payment was made t_P. This provides a measure of the total period of time during which traders could have been exposed to exchange risk, as well as illuminating the minimum possible period within which the trade balance can be expected to respond positively to an exchange rate change. We term this the 'contract period'.

One other element of a firm's environment that influences its trade financing practices consists of the exchange control regulations to which it is subject. In the United Kingdom these were quite strict. In general UK exporters were required to convert any foreign currency they received into sterling immediately. The only exception concerned firms that received exchange control permission to open a foreign currency (or 'hold') account, which could be granted where a firm had sufficiently regular export/import business. Up to 10,000 such accounts were approved (with some firms maintaining more than one account, in more than one currency). Firms with such accounts were generally authorised to credit certain classes of foreign currency receipts to their accounts, but were obliged once a month to sell to a bank for sterling any excess of their balances over known payments due during the following month. In addition to the rule requiring immediate conversion of foreign currency receipts into sterling, UK exporters were limited to granting export credit for a maximum period of 6 months, unless a longer period was specifically approved by the Bank of England or the contract was insured by ECGD. Exporters could sell their expected receipts forward immediately they fixed the date that a foreign currency payment will fall due.

A UK importer who had to pay his supplier in foreign currency could buy that currency only when he was about to make the payment. There is again, of course, the limited exception that applied to those firms that were authorised to maintain hold accounts. Importers could take forward cover as long in advance of an expected payment as they wished, and up to 6 months beyond the expected date of importing the goods. They were not restricted as to the length of export credit that they accepted, but, except with the specific permission of the Bank of England, they could not pay for any import in advance of its shipment to the UK. Such permission was normally given only for certain imports of raw materials and capital goods.

These regulations allowed very little scope for leading and lagging by UK residents varying the timing of purchases or sales of foreign currency relative to the date of payment or receipt. Holders of foreign currency accounts had some flexibility in this direction, by running down the end-month balances below the permitted maxima and by varying the proportions of their receipts and payments passed through the accounts within the month, but the total potential effects of such operations were believed to be of fairly modest size. There may also, of course, have been some evasion of the exchange control regulations; by the nature of illegal transactions one cannot quantify this factor, but the exchange control regulations were strictly enforced and the authorities did not regard evasion as a serious problem. It follows that the principal source of leads and lags should be sought in variations in the timing of receipts and payments.

It may be noted that the exchange control regulations applied to all firms legally resident in the UK, including the local branches of foreign-owned multinationals.

1.2 Micro-economic incentives

As noted above, there are four degrees of freedom in the financial side of trade transaction; choice of the invoice currency, whether to seek forward cover, the method of settlement, and the length of credit to be allowed and the proportion of it to be taken up. In the present section we examine what light microeconomic theory can throw on the decisions that rationally-managed firms might be expected to reach on these issues. Our discussion is based in substantial part on the analysis contained in an important new book by Ronald McKinnon (1979).

McKinnon analyses trade between independent firms, i.e. excluding that between branches of the same multinational corporations (MNC) and assumes that both trading partners are located in countries with a convertible currency. He starts from the premise that firms engaged in foreign trade seek certainty in terms of their domestic currency – a premise particularly appropriate for a country such as the UK where exchange controls required that foreign earnings be converted into sterling. He argues that one should expect trade financing practices to differ radically between two categories of goods, labelled 'tradables I' and 'tradables II'. The first comprises products with some degree of product differentiation whose price is set by their producers, while the second group consists of those goods whose prices are determined by demand and supply on world-wide markets.[4] Cars are a typical example of tradables I, while wheat is a typical example of tradables II. More generally, the distinction is very close to that between manufactures and primary products.

A producer of tradables I has costs that are largely specified in terms of his domestic currency. Hence he can reduce his risks by setting a price in terms of his domestic currency, and allowing inventories rather than price to vary so as to clear the market in the short run. In order to fix price in terms of his domestic currency he has to invoice his exports in terms of his own currency, which of course throws the burden of exchange-rate risk on to the importer. There are two main ways in which the importer may be able to reduce this risk: by gaining some freedom to choose the timing of his payment, and by covering his position in the forward market. (McKinnon also analyses the possibility of importers covering their position by buying the relevant foreign currency spot prior to payment becoming due, but UK exchange control regulations precluded adoption of this strategy by British importers.) Where the exporter has sufficient confidence in his trading partner, one would expect him to be willing to give his partner the advantage of buying on open account, with the associated freedom to select the time when payment will be made, rather than tying him down by a formal contract to make payment on a specified date. One would also expect to find considerable forward covering in this type of trade.[5] However, one should not necessarily expect to find all transactions covered (even partially) forward; first, because traders will sometimes wish to hold open positions for essentially speculative reasons, and, second, because transactions costs (buy/sell spreads) are wider in the forward than in the spot market, so that the period for which the risk is borne may be too brief to make the extra expense worth while.

The situation is very different for tradables II. Exporters are price takers who do not have the market power to fix domestic currency prices, but simply have to accept the going international price in terms of the currency in which the market operates. They have no particular incentive to invoice in their own currency, since (unlike the producer of tradables I) the value of their inventories cannot be protected by an administered price. On the other hand, importers of tradables II have an interest in being invoiced in the same currency as other traders in the same product. The reason is that this enables them to offset 'exchange risk' (the risk that the firm bears through having an open position in foreign exchange) by 'price risk' (the risk that the price of the goods that the firm has in inventory may change).[6] For example, a 10% depreciation of sterling can be expected to raise the sterling price of wheat by about 11.1%, i.e. to leave its dollar price unaffected, except to the surely second-order extent that the sterling depreciation alters the world balance between demand and supply. A British importer who has already contracted to buy wheat at a fixed dollar price therefore has his exchange risk neutralised by price risk; he does not need forward cover. There are therefore significant gains if transactions are invoiced in terms of 'international money', or what is often referred to as a 'vehicle currency', and competitive pressures force exporters to offer such invoices. Where a commodity is traded on a central international market, like the Chicago wheat market or the London tea market, one might furthermore expect to find the vehicle currency used being the currency of the country where the market is located. Since all the major commodity markets are located in either the United States or Britain, the 'vehicle currencies' may be taken as the dollar and sterling.

However, where the vehicle currency is not the exporter's own currency, he bears exchange risk by invoicing in the vehicle currency. Any exporter in this position has an incentive to avoid adding to this risk by allowing the importer to choose the exact timing of payment. Hence the exporter is less likely to give credit, and when he does this is more likely to be through a formal instrument payable in a precisely-specified number of days. This also aids the exporter in covering his position forward if he so desires.

Consider now how these conclusions, all of which were drawn from McKinnon's work centred on trade between independent firms, need to be modified in the case of trade between two branches of an MNC. The essential difference between the two cases is that, for the MNC as a whole, it does not matter which branch bears the exchange risk. Thus one would not expect multinationals exporting tradables I to another branch of the same corporation to display the same anxiety to invoice in domestic currency as in the case of transactions between independent firms. On the other hand, the incentives for invoicing tradables II are unaffected, since the importer bears no 'net exchange risk' (i.e., price risk offsets exchange risk) in any event.

The fact that when a multinational is trading internally it does not matter (except perhaps for distortions caused by taxation) which branch of the firm bears the exchange risk does not mean that multinationals are indifferent to exchange rate changes or will never take forward cover. On the contrary, if they come to believe that one currency is going to depreciate relative to another, they have exactly the same incentive as any other agent to shift funds from the depreciating to the appreciating currency. What is special about the position of an MNC is not the incentives it faces but its ability to respond to those incentives, in particular by leading and lagging trade payments between branches in countries with currencies expected to depreciate and appreciate. Exchange control, unless it be Draconian, cannot prevent the acceleration of a payment due to a branch in a strong-currency country by a branch in a weak-currency country, nor the retardation of payments in the opposite direction. (There is no conflict between the proposition that the currency of invoice is irrelevant and the proposition that profits can be made by leading and lagging: the gain to the MNC *as a whole* depends on the timing of the payments, but not on which currency the transaction is denominated in.) The desire to maximise opportunities for profiting through leading and lagging is a factor, additional to administrative simplicity, and without the offsetting risk of bad faith by the partner, which would make one expect to find intra-MNC transactions settled on open account. Alternatively, if the forward rate does not reflect the spot rate that the MNC expects to see in the future (either because it takes a different view to other market operators or, no doubt more important, because of central bank support for the forward rate), it may be able to achieve the same objective by buying forward cover. This will tend to be particularly attractive if the branches' respective liquidity positions make further variations in the timing of payment inconvenient. In times when no dramatic rate change is expected, however, a multinational trading internally would not be expected to take forward cover. Since our data were taken from a period of reasonable tranquility in the exchange market, we did not expect to find multinationals trading internally in tradables I with forward cover.

Consider finally in what ways the previous conclusions would need to be modified in the case of trade with a country which has an inconvertible currency. The fact that it is inconvertible means that there is no market in that currency abroad. An exporter selling to such a country could therefore not rely on being easily able to convert earnings in that currency back into his home currency; hence the presumption that he will invoice in his home currency (for tradables I) or in a vehicle currency (for tradables II) is strengthened. Conversely, the fact that there is no market in such a currency accessible in their own country means that it would be inconvenient to firms that imported from such a country if their purchases were invoiced in the currency of the exporter. Hence one would expect to find that imports from such countries, while following the normal rule in the case of tradables II, would deviate from the normal pattern in the case of tradables I; in order to compete, the exporter would be obliged to forgo the advantages of invoicing in his home currency. If his own currency is pegged to a vehicle currency, there would be some convenience to him in using that as the invoice currency; but, since that convenience gain would presumably be less than that normally gained by an exporter through invoicing in his home currency, one might expect to find invoicing in the importer's currency (which is the most attractive policy to his clients) more frequent.

The preceding discussion contains a series of specific and testable hypotheses about the choices that will be made with regard to the first three of the four issues listed at the start of this section. The exception is the length of credit to be allowed and the proportion of that credit that is taken up; we cover this topic, in a largely descriptive way, in Chapter 5. For convenience we summarise our hypotheses on the remaining three issues below.

Currency of invoice

Hypothesis I. Tradables I exported to an independent firm from a country with a convertible currency will be invoiced in the exporter's currency.

Hypothesis II. Tradables II will be invoiced in a vehicle currency (dollars or sterling).

Hypothesis IIA. The vehicle currency used for invoicing commodities traded on an international market will be the currency of the country where the international market for the commodity in question is located.

Hypothesis III. Tradables I exported to another branch of the same MNC are less likely to be invoiced in the home currency of the exporter than are tradables I exports sold to an independent firm.

Hypothesis IV. Tradables I imported from countries with inconvertible currencies will be invoiced in either sterling or dollars, with the sterling-invoiced proportion being higher than in imports from countries with convertible currencies.

Use of the forward market

Hypothesis V. Importers of tradables I invoiced in a foreign currency are more likely to cover forward than are importers of tradables II invoiced in a foreign currency.

Hypothesis VI. Except when the central bank is supporting the forward rate, intra-MNC transactions are less likely to be covered forward than are transactions between independent firms.

Method of settlement

Hypothesis VII. Sales on open account or similar terms, other than within an MNC, will be more common (a) for transactions invoiced in the exporter's currency, and (b) the longer the two partners to the transactions have been trading with one another.

Hypothesis VIII. All transactions between the branches of a MNC will be settled on open account.

These eight hypotheses will be subjected to empirical tests, on the basis of the data that we collected, in Chapters 4 and 5. It should perhaps be remarked that they are far from being trivial hypotheses. Indeed, in some respects the literature until recently tended to convey a quite different view of the financing practices prevalent in foreign trade. In this view, which happens to have been represented among other places in one of McKinnon's earlier papers (1969) and is perpetuated in the recent work of Alec Chrystal (1978), international traders are pictured as wanting to hold internationally-acceptable monies in order to finance their international transactions much as domestic agents want to hold domestic money. The picture one is there shown is of trade being predominantly invoiced and settled in one or two vehicle currencies, with traders finding it convenient to hold working balances of those currencies in order to make and receive payments. The 'vehicle currency hypothesis', as it has become known, postulates that there will be only one or two vehicle currencies because of economies of scale in the holding and use of money; total money inventories can be lower, for the same level of security, if everyone uses the same money. What Grassman (1973b) has called the 'symmetry hypothesis', which is essentially our Hypothesis I except that he applied it to all goods rather than just to tradables I, contends that the role of vehicle currencies is far more limited than postulated by the vehicle currency hypothesis. Just how extensive this role is will be another subject on which we shall attempt to shed light in the following chapters.

2

A SUMMARY OF PREVIOUS STUDIES

Until recently the literature on the financing procedures of foreign trade was scattered and impressionistic. By far the most prolific writer on the subject was Paul Einzig, who touched on the topic again and again in a long series of books, and indeed devoted two of them primarily to the subject (1962, 1968). While eschewing quantitative statements, which he argued were liable to be misleading because attitudes toward covering exchange risk changed suddenly and frequently in response to market developments, he described what he believed to be prevailing practices and noted major changes over time. His early writings reflected the dominance of sterling, especially in British trade but also as an important vehicle for third-country trade, while in more recent years he commented on the decline in the use of sterling and the associated growth of what he called 'foreign exchange mindedness' (meaning a willingness to invoice or be invoiced in foreign currencies) on the part of British traders.

While Einzig's writings provide useful background material even now, and are almost unique as a historical record, his refusal to quantify limits the usefulness of his work. In our view, the fact (if it is a fact) that practices are liable to abrupt change does not eliminate the value of quantification; on the contrary, it increases the need for quantitative estimates, especially those that can throw light on the scope for, and speed of, changes in practices. To judge by the number of other recent contributors to the literature who have attempted quantification, it would seem that we are not alone in this view.

This new branch of the literature was sparked by Sven Grassman's pioneering study (1973a). Although this was antedated by a paper by Bent Hansen and Thora Nilsson (1960) and other Scandinavian-language papers by these two authors, it was undoubtedly Grassman's use of a large-scale random sample of 1968 Swedish trade transactions that began to lay a solid base of knowledge and revealed empirical regularities of sufficient interest to provoke the attention of others. These include not only those whose work will be summarised in this chapter, but also Ronald McKinnon whose theoretical work was noted in the preceding chapter.

This chapter is divided into four sections, which correspond to the four issues identified at the beginning of Section 1.2: invoice currency, forward cover, method of settlement, and length and elasticity of the period of credit. In each section we present the principal conclusions of past studies in the form of tables, in which the results of different studies are listed in the chronological order of publication. Where our investigation has yielded comparable figures, we add these results to the table for ease of comparison. More detail is, of course, provided in subsequent chapters.

2.1 The currency of invoice

In the light of the microeconomic analysis in Section 1.2, we regard the most interesting aspect of this question as the breakdown between the seller's currency, the buyers' currency, and a third currency. Unfortunately the more common way in which to present these data has been in terms of the proportion invoiced in dollars, pounds, DM, etc. This traditional classification scheme makes it easy to identify exports invoiced in the exporter's currency and imports invoiced in the importer's currency, but generally impossible to make a further breakdown, e.g. between exports invoiced in the buyer's currency and those invoiced in a third currency. However, it is sometimes possible to get a minimum estimate of the proportion of trade invoiced in the dollar in its role as a third currency, which will usually not be far below the true figure, by subtracting the proportion of the country's trade that is with the United States from the proportion of its trade invoiced in dollars. Despite this, the data presented in Table 2.1, which is an attempt to draw together comparable data from a number of sources, are distinctly patchy.

The earliest (but unpublished) study of the subject was made in the IMF in 1969 by our former colleague, Fred Hirsch. This was based on conversations with central bankers, who had themselves in some cases used exchange control data in forming their estimates. The French data are particularly interesting as revealing estimates of the impact that currency uncertainties had on invoicing practices: French exporters were estimated to have reduced their franc invoicing by over a third before they were forced to revert to more normal practices by the Draconian exchange controls introduced in November 1968 following the Bonn Conference.

Fieleke's study (1971) of US–Canadian trade obviously dealt with a very special case. His figure is included for comprehensiveness.

Grassman (1973a) provided the first solid empirical results. His major conclusion was, of course, the 'symmetry theorem'; that by and large exports are invoiced in the exporter's currency. He found some fairly systematic deviations from this, however. The most pronounced of these

Table 2.1. *Percentage of value of trade invoiced in seller's, buyer's and third currencies*

			Exports invoiced in:				*Imports* invoiced in:			
Source	Country	Year	Seller's currency	Buyer's currency	Third currency	US $ as third currency	Seller's currency	Buyer's currency	Third currency	US $ as third currency
Hirsch	France[a]	1967	c.50					37		
		Jan–Sep. 1968	c.32					33		
		1969	50?					33+		
	Germany	1969	60–80							
	UK	1969	c.85					45[b]		
Fieleke (1971)	US/Canada	1970–71	23 out of 123 US firms had contracts expressed in Canadian dollars							
Grassman (1973a)	Sweden	1968	66.1	24.9	9.0	5.6+	58.8	25.8	15.4	13.2
Grassman (1973b)	Denmark	1971	41			14+		19		17+
Magee (1974)	US imports from Germany	1971						27		
	US imports from Germany	1973						12		
	US imports from Japan	1971						61		
	US imports from Japan	1973						72		
Grassman (1976)	Sweden	1973	67.4					25.7		
Brittan (1977)	UK	1977						c.30		
Page (1977)	Austria	1973	46.7							
		1975	54.7			7.6+		24.7		13.5+
	Belgium	1971	46.2							
		1973	48.9							
		1975	50.4							
		1976	47.7			7.3+		25.4		18.8+

	Denmark[c]	1971	41							
		1973	52							
		1975	54							
		1976	54			6.2+		23		17.8+
	France	1972	59.4							
		1974	68.3							
		1976	68.3	24.1		5.5+		31.5		22.6
	Germany	1972	84.1							
		1974	88.3							
		1976	86.9			0+		42.0		23.6+
	Netherlands	1968	42.3[d]					23.5[d]		
		1973	45.3					26.2[d]		
		1976	50.2			10.2+		31.4		12.9+
Department of Trade (1978)	UK	April 1976	80	12	9	8				
		Oct.–Nov. 1976	73	15	12	12				
		May 1977	70	15	15	14				
Present study	UK	1975	75.9	17.3	6.8	6.0	50.9	30.3	18.8	17.0

Notes:
[a] Figures refer to trade outside franc zone.
[b] Non-sterling area imports
[c] Goods and services
[d] Figure derived from Van Nieuwkerk (1979) who evidently drew on the same basic source as Page but had access to additional data.
+Signifies that this is a minimum estimate derived by subtracting trade with the US from total dollar invoicing.

was geographical: exports to, as well as imports from the 'reserve-currency countries',[1] were predominantly invoiced in the dollar or the pound, while in contrast to this the currency of the trading partner dropped out of the picture entirely in trade with Eastern Europe and the 'rest of the world' (roughly equal to Japan and the LDCs). Another exception was that fuel was predominantly invoiced in a third currency, principally sterling. A third was associated with size of transaction; small export transactions were more prone to be invoiced in Swedish kronor than were large ones, but this at least partly reflected the invoicing of oil and timber in third currencies. In 1973b he added some data on Danish invoicing practices.

Magee (1974) studied a sample of US import transactions from Germany and Japan in 1971 and 1973. He found German exports to be predominantly invoiced in Deutsche Marks(DM), with the proportion invoiced in dollars falling sharply between the two years; this is not surprising in view of the risk that German exporters by then knew they were running in invoicing in dollars. Japanese exports, in contrast, tended to be invoiced predominantly in dollars (and this tendency was accentuated between 1971 and 1973, despite the strength of the yen in that period). In this they followed the pattern that Grassman's work had suggested was typical of the LDCs.

Grassman's 1976 study of 1973 Swedish trade found little change from the invoicing pattern of 1968, except for the decline of the pound sterling in both the invoicing of British imports from Sweden and in its third-currency role (where it was largely displaced by the dollar and DM). In other words, it appears that between 1968 and 1973 the pound became a normal European currency, at least from this point of view.

Brittan quoted an estimate made by A. G. Horsnail, a London-based consultant economist.

Page (1977) assembled the figures that are now being compiled by a number of European countries, for as far back as she was able.[2] It will be seen that the pattern of exports being invoiced predominantly in the exporter's currency, with the use of the importer's currency also being important, is general, at least within Europe. Two other regularities stand out. First, there is a pronounced tendency for the extent of domestic currency invoicing on both sides of the account to vary positively with the size of the economy. Second, there is a fairly consistent time trend toward greater use of the seller's currency in the invoicing of exports.

The Department of Trade has now started collecting figures on the invoicing of UK exports (but not imports) on a regular basis. The results of the first three such enquiries are shown in Table 2.1. Contrary to the general time trend toward domestic currency invoicing of exports noted above for most European countries, these data show a sharp drop in sterling invoicing, which was particularly pronounced during the period of sterling's weakness between the Spring and Autumn of 1976. It was suggested by Page that this might result from a random fluctuation or a fault in the surveys rather than a genuine change in behaviour, but the further small decline in sterling invoicing subsequently found in May 1977 suggests that the decline is probably real.

Our own study yielded figures that are generally consistent with the picture revealed by other studies, although, since they were taken from a period prior to the apparent decline in sterling invoicing of exports, they shed no light on the reality of this decline and the apparent associated growth in dollar invoicing.

Previous studies have also yielded some detail on the currency of invoice classified in ways other than by overall use of the seller's currency, buyer's currency, and a third currency. The most popular classification scheme has been by listing the various currencies – dollar, pound, DM, etc. We do not regard this classification scheme as of sufficient usefulness to merit reproducing the results of such studies, but those interested can find compilations of this type in Grassman (1973a, Table 2.2, p. 23; 1973b; 1976), Page (1977, Table 4, p. 81) and Van Nieuwkerk (1979, Table 1).

A second basis of classification is in relation to the geographical location of the trading partner. The studies by Fieleke and Magee, noted in Table 2.1, were confined to trade with one and two trading partners respectively. In addition both Grassman and the DoT provided data on this basis: Grassman's qualitative results were noted in the text above. The results of the Department of Trade surveys, Grassman's study on the export side, a French survey quoted by Page, and our own study on the export side, are summarised in Table 2.2. The notable features are that exports to other European countries follow the overall pattern (which is of course not surprising given the large share of these markets in total exports); that exports to the United States generally made far greater use of the buyer's currency than did those to any other area; and that exports to the centrally-planned economies make negligible use of the buyer's currency. It may also be noted that Van Nieuwkerk has reported the impression that the trade of the Netherlands with both the United States and Germany is overwhelmingly invoiced in dollars and DM respectively on both sides of the account, thus suggesting that the DM may be emerging as a new vehicle currency that will qualify the pattern of symmetry characteristic of intra-European relations.

The third basis of classification is by commodity. Magee found some definite patterns in this respect: organic chemicals were invoiced in the exporter's currency by both Germany and Japan, while both invoiced steel in dollars. The Germans invoiced cars and components in DM while the Japanese invoiced in dollars. Surprisingly, the pattern was

Table 2.2. *Currency of invoicing by market*

(*Percentages by value*)

	Date	Currency used: Exporter's	Currency used: Importer's	US dollar as third currency
Exports to EEC				
by France	1976	58.0	38.3	4.0
by Sweden	1968	61	33	
by UK	April 1976	79	15	5
	Oct. 1976	69	21	10
	May 1977	63	19	16
	1975	50.8	41.9	6.8
Exports to other Western Europe countries				
by France	1976	55.1	32.1	10.9
by Sweden	1968	84.4	11.4	
by UK	April 1976	84	8	7
	Oct. 1976	81	11	6
	May 1977	67	10	22
	1975	86.1	11.7	2.0
Exports to United States				
by France	1976	42.8	56.6	n.a.
by Sweden	1968	35.3	64.5	n.a.
by UK	April 1976	70	30	n.a.
	Oct. 1976	51	49	n.a.
	May 1977	55	45	n.a.
	1975	83.4	16.6	n.a.
Exports to Japan				
by France	1976	75.6	10.6	13.5
by UK	April 1976	70	0	30
	Oct. 1976	73	19	8
	May 1977	74	0	26
Exports to centrally planned economies				
by Sweden	1968	87.8	0	
by UK	April 1976	76	0	24
	Oct. 1976	100	0	0
	May 1977	94	0	6
	1975	99.9	0	0.1

Notes: There are slight deviations in geographical coverage in some cases. No entry implies not known; n.a. = not applicable; 0 = none.

Sources: France, Centre d'Observation Economique, as quoted in Page (1977, Table 2); Sweden, Grassman (1973a, 1976), as quoted in Page, *idem.*; UK, 1976–77, Department of Trade (1978, p. 275); UK 1975, the survey reported in the present study.

partly reversed for tyres where Germany invoiced in dollars while Japan used a mixture of dollar and yen invoicing.

The more comprehensive studies undertaken by Grassman and the Department of Trade are again summarised, along with some of our own results on the export side, in Table 2.3. There seems to be a fairly clear tendency for exporter-currency invoicing to be more predominant in the more highly manufactured articles, especially engineering products.

We conclude this section by noting two estimates of the proportion of

Table 2.3. *Share of exporter's currency in invoicing by commodity*

(*Percentages by value*)

	Sweden	United Kingdom			
	1968	April 1976	October 1976	May 1977	1975
Food, beverages, tobacco	49	73	67	78	81
Fuels and basic materials	30	78	65	42	82
Chemicals	62	75	65	52	49
Textiles	73	69	66	77	
Metals and articles of metal	64	69	59	59	
Electrical machinery	72	91	76	80	70
Other machinery	83	82	88	89	
Transport equipment	77	95	90	89	92
Other manufactured goods	65	79	72	56	

Note: There are discrepancies in classification that prevent our quoting figures from our own study (final column) for all commodities.
Sources: Sweden: Grassman (1973a, 1976), as quoted by Page (1977, Table 2); UK, 1976–77: Department of Trade (1978, Table 2, p. 275); UK, 1975: the survey reported in the present study.

total world trade that is invoiced in dollars. Cohen (1971, p. 18) reported, on the basis of his discussions in the City of London in 1969, that at least one third of world trade was thought to be invoiced and transacted in dollars (and probably another 20 to 25% in sterling). Grassman (1973b), on the basis of the somewhat firmer evidence provided by extrapolating the results of his Swedish and Danish studies to other countries, estimated that in 1970 the proportion of world trade invoiced in dollars was some 26%, as against a US share of world trade of 14%. In view of the shift toward invoicing in the exporter's own currency shown in Table 2.1, it is probable that the percentage invoiced in dollars is now somewhat lower.

2.2 Use of the forward market

Forward markets, in short maturities, have a large and fairly steady volume of trading as between the principal currencies – the US dollar, sterling, DM, and the Swiss franc. Markets in the French and Belgian francs, the Canadian dollar, the guilder and the yen are less active, although volume on the yen market is growing rapidly. In such other currencies as the Australian dollar, the Austrian schilling, the rand, the lira, the Swedish krona and the Danish and Norwegian krone, the market is substantially less active, but there is never any difficulty in obtaining cover of the shorter maturities. In terms of maturity, the market in the three month maturity is generally the most active, although on increasingly frequent occasions the six month maturity may experience comparable volume. The one year market, while still quite active, is markedly less so than the three and six month markets. Beyond that, in terms of both maturity and currency, markets thin rapidly. That is, banks are unwilling to assume open positions and transactions are few and far between, so that completion of a transaction will depend on the intermediary bank finding a matching transaction, and that will usually take time. Nevertheless, if you want to cover the Finnish markka two years forward in terms of the Spanish peseta, you may manage to, eventually.

Although forward markets are quite active and have been analysed intensively by economists from the time of Keynes' *Tract* onwards, there has been some debate in recent years as to whether they in fact play a very significant role in relation to trade transactions (as opposed to in relation to short-term capital movements). We therefore again assemble in a systematic way, in Table 2.4, a number of estimates of the proportion of trade that is covered in the forward market. It is important to be clear as to whether such estimates refer to *total* exports or imports, or only to those invoiced in foreign currency; the proportion covered on the latter basis will be higher, and often much higher, than on the former basis. For example, Grassman's estimate that in 1968 'only' 9.8% of British exports were covered forward is in fact equivalent to Hirsch's figure of about 50% of those exports which were invoiced in foreign currency, since about 80% of British exports were believed to be invoiced in sterling at that time. (This consistency is not surprising since both estimates have a common source.)

The first reasonably systematic, though hitherto unpublished, estimates of the extent to which forward cover was sought were assembled by Fred Hirsch on the basis of his conversations with central bankers in 1969. The general picture that emerged was of limited use of the forward market in what were, perhaps optimistically, referred to as 'normal' times, i.e. in periods without speculative pressure; both French and German estimates were that only around 10% of the trade invoiced in foreign currency would be covered in such periods. However, as Paul Einzig had conjectured, this proportion was very sensitive indeed to the speculative atmosphere, and was believed to have risen to 70% or more for both French imports and German exports in the hysterical atmosphere that led up to the Bonn Conference in November 1968. (The reported rise in covering of French exports in early 1968 looks distinctly odd, although the decline reported later in the year is what one would expect.) Similarly, UK experience was of an average cover on non-sterling invoiced imports of about 25% over the (never 'normal') years 1965–68, but with sharp rises at such crisis times as July 1966, November 1967, and November 1968 – rises made possible without a corresponding increase in covering on the other side of the market by the support given

Table 2.4. *Estimates of the proportion of trade covered in the forward market*

(percentages)

			Exports		Imports	
Source	Country	Year	Total	Foreign currency invoiced	Total	Foreign currency invoiced
Hirsch	France	1959		6		10
		1966		13		10
		1967		20		12
		1968		36		33
		July–Nov. 1968		below 20		70+
	Germany	Sep.–Nov. 1968		70?		low
	UK	1968		c. 50		25
Fieleke (1971)	US/Canada	1970/71	3 out of 23 US firms with contracts in Canadian dollars took forward cover			
Grassman (1973a)[a]	UK	1968	9.8		13.4	
	France	1969	0.4		0.3	
	Sweden	1969	6.8	(20.1)	6.0	(8.1)
	Belgium	1970	5.8		5.6	
	Denmark	1970	1.4		6.3	
Grassman (1976)	Sweden	post-March 1973	Use of forward market more than doubled			
Brittan (1977)	UK	Early 1977				almost one third
Van Nieuwkerk (1979)[b]	Netherlands	1968	18.4	31.9	14.3	18.7
		1973	22.5	41.1	32.4	43.9
		1976	22.7	45.6	31.6	46.1
Present study	UK	Feb. 1975	3.7	15.5	25.3	36.3

Notes:
[a] Exports or imports of goods and services
[b] Exports or imports of goods, services and capital
Other figures refer to exports or imports of goods

by the Bank of England to the forward rate. (However, this support was withdrawn for most of 1968, and it was the substantial discount on forward sterling that this caused – a discount that widened at times close to 2% on 3 month forward sterling, equivalent to nearly 8% per annum – that tempted exporters invoiced in foreign currency into the market in such numbers. A bird in the hand, in the form of a substantial premium, was wisely judged worth two in the bush, in the form of the second sterling devaluation that never came.)

Fieleke cited several reasons as to why only 3 out of 23 firms had covered their exchange exposure. The most common was that the amounts involved were 'too small', while some said that they did not know enough about the market. Two noted that they did not cover because they were dealing with subsidiaries; since this was a period of floating rates with little intervention of the Bank of Canada, this is consistent with our conjecture (page 13) that such transactions are covered only when there is an opportunity to speculate against a central bank. As Fieleke notes, saying that the amounts were 'too small' implies an expectation about the likely extent of exchange rate variation, and does not rule out the possibility that the extent of covering, which he thought surprisingly low, might rise should the exchange rate prove more variable. However, comparison of Fieleke's result with other studies makes one wonder whether the proportion really was unusually low.

Grassman compiled figures for five European countries on the basis of information provided by four central banks and extracted from the Annual Report of a fifth. His principal conclusion was that the percentages of trade covered forward were extremely low, and did not justify the attention given to the forward market in describing and analysing trade financing practices. He may, however, have somewhat overstated this point. First, he expressed his results as a proportion of total trade rather than of trade exposed to exchange risk: the effect of using the alternative base is illustrated in the Swedish case by the figures in parentheses, which have been calculated on the assumption that Grassman's results on the currency of invoice in 1968 held good in 1969 as well. Second, he quoted the derisorily-low French figures with no warning that these were not a testimony to the lack of interest of French importers in protecting themselves against the near-certainty of a franc devaluation, but rather a testimony to the beliefs of exchange controllers (who no doubt provided the underlying figures) as to how effective they think they can be when they get really tough. (Forward cover of more than one month was virtually banned in 1969, and even 1 month cover was restricted to some 25 to 30% of imports.)

Grassman's updated study (1976) shows a sharp rise in the use of the forward market by Swedish firms after the move to generalised floating in March 1973. This is, of course, what economists had long predicted would happen. Even so, the proportion of trade that is exposed to exchange risk and not covered forward remains quite high. It may be that trade within the snake did not share in the move toward greater forward covering; an empirical examination of this point would be fascinating. Grassman noted that large contracts and long credit periods were particularly likely to be covered forward, which – except for very long credit periods, where the thinness of the market may hamper covering – is what one would expect.

Brittan's estimate is again drawn from the work of A. G. Horsnail.

Van Nieuwkerk's estimates show a much higher proportion of Dutch trade to have been covered than occurred in any other country except during times of crisis. (His own figures are expressed as a proportion of trade invoiced in foreign currency that is covered.) There may be some upward bias in his estimates, since they were derived from stock data of average outstanding forward commitments by assuming (a) that capital movements are no more likely to be covered forward than is trade, and (b) that the average forward contract was of three months duration, which may be on the low side. (Hirsch stated that in the UK about two thirds of forward covering by number of contracts was for three months, but with sufficient other maturities (notably six months) to raise the average, by value, to about four months.) Nevertheless, this evidence does suggest that a freely-available, well-functioning forward market, such as exists in the Netherlands, will lead to a substantial proportion of trade being covered. And if Van Nieuwkerk is correct in the belief he expresses that trade invoiced in DM and Belgian francs is largely left uncovered, presumably because of the close association of the guilder with these two currencies in the European snake, the proportion of other trade covered must be quite high.

Van Nieuwkerk's paper is also notable for its description, and to some extent quantification, of alternative methods of protecting against exchange risk. Apart from invoicing in domestic currency and covering in the forward market, he mentions the following possibilities:

1. Including an exchange rate clause in the contract, which allows possible exchange losses to be charged to the other party. Since this is more disadvantageous to the trading partner than invoicing in domestic currency (it presents the latter with additional costs if his currency depreciates without giving him the advantages if it appreciates), it is not surprising that this method appears to be of negligible importance.
2. Seeking cover from an insurance company on export contracts too long (over two years) and/or too large for the forward market. He estimated that this method was used on less than 1% of Dutch exports.
3. Transferring export claims to a bank or factoring company that undertakes to collect the debts and assumes the exchange risks in the process. This practice is believed to be rare.
4. Compensating risks internally by maintaining a balanced position between debts and claims denominated in various currencies. No information on the importance of this technique was available.
5. Compensating exchange risks externally by, for example, buying foreign currency necessary for future settlements spot at an earlier date and holding it. (This technique was not permitted by exchange control regulations in the UK.) He estimated, on the basis of some assumptions that would seem subject to a wide margin of uncertainty, that imports covered in this way had increased from some 8% of total imports in 1968 to some 17% in 1976.

6. Leading and lagging, which he did not quantify, and which in any case cannot reduce risks to an extent comparable to that of the other techniques.

Notable for its absence from his list is the offsetting of exchange risk by price risk. Nevertheless, he concluded that at least 45% of Dutch imports and 60% of Dutch exports in 1968, and more than three quarters of both in 1976, were protected against exchange risk by one of the techniques that he had quantified (including invoicing in guilders, but not in DM or Belgian francs).

2.3 The method of settlement

It is remarkable how little is known of the quantitative importance of the various methods of settlement. Grassman's pioneering study contained details regarding Swedish trade in 1968, but, unlike his work on the currency of invoice, this has until now provoked no imitators.

A revised presentation of Grassman's aggregate results, classified along the lines suggested by our discussion in Chapter 1 is contained in Table 2.5, together with a summary of our results as reported more fully in Chapter 5. Grassman drew attention to the very high proportion of Swedish trade, on both sides of the account, which used variable-credit techniques, specifically open account. This rather unexpected finding seemed to go a long way toward explaining the facility with which firms could lead and lag when they so chose. Our own results suggest that there is in this respect a very considerable difference between the practices typical in Swedish and in British trade. Formal instruments of payment still seem to be used for the bulk of British exports and also to

Table 2.5. *Methods of settlement used in Swedish and British foreign trade*

(*Percentages of value*)

	Exports		Imports	
	Sweden 1968	UK 1975	Sweden 1968	UK 1975
No credit	25.2	38.1	14.4	41.8
whereof advance[a]	0.6	0.1	2.3	insignificant
Fixed credit	17.9	32.9	13.9	14.8
whereof instalments[b]	11.8	21.3	6.0	2.9
Variable credit	55.0	28.9	70.2	43.4
whereof consignment	2.1	1.8	1.7	0.9
Other	1.9	–	1.5	–

Notes:

[a] Whole amount paid

[b] Including advance instalment payments

Sources: Sweden: Grassman (1973a, Table 2.4, p. 28); UK: Questionnaire survey

play a substantially larger role in the financing of British than of Swedish imports.

Grassman also presented some breakdown of method of settlement (basically open account versus other) by trading partner and size of transaction. There was a reasonably clear tendency for open account to become progressively less frequent as the 'political and geographic distance' from Sweden increased, and some tendency for it to decrease as the size of transaction increased. He also stated that MNCs tend to settle on open account.

2.4 Length and elasticity of the period of credit

It seems to be widely believed that during the last 20 years or so there has been a general lengthening of the credit terms between international traders. Factors that have been cited as contributing to this include a general increase in confidence and trust among traders, a trend towards buyers' markets, the spread of MNCs, and a resort to easier credit terms as a competitive weapon, particularly in trade in large capital goods.

Once again, we seek in this section to draw together the results of previous studies. We also note a related discussion about the relationship between trade credit and the balance of payments residual.

Statistics on the outstanding stock of trade credits are available for a number of countries from published sources. Such statistics have been quoted by, for example, Einzig (1968, Appendix). Uggla (1970), and Grassman (1973a, Chapter 3). Grassman noted that the non-financial sector's total foreign credits and debts were of very similar magnitude and generally rose in parallel, but were of such size relative to the central bank's official reserves – both assets and liabilities were almost four times as large as the Riksbank's reserves in 1970 – that even small variations in the relationship between the credits extended and received had major implications for the development of official reserves.

In the Swedish case Grassman was able to show that trade credits dominated the assets and liabilities of the non-financial sector. In Britain this is not the case, as the statistics on the UK foreign portfolio at the end of 1975 show (Table 2.6). Both direct investment and the Euro market activities of the banking system are far more important in Britain, on both sides of the account. Nevertheless, even excluding commercial bills discounted (i.e. trade credit extended abroad by the banking sector), trade credit both given and taken was almost as large as the official reserves of £2,700 millions.

Such statistics on the stock of outstanding trade credit have been used to calculate average credit periods, by comparing the stocks of credits and debits with the flows of exports and imports respectively. The first

Table 2.6. *The UK foreign portfolio* 1975

(£ *millions*)

	Assets	Liabilities
Direct investment	23,400	14,095
Banking sector	63,384	65,287
of which, commercial bills discounted	4,391	–
Trade credit	2,452	2,392
Miscellaneous private sector	165	–
Public sector: monetary	2,700	4,365
other	2,165	6,365
Total	94,265	92,505

Source: Bank of England *Quarterly Bulletin*, June 1976, Table E pp. 210–11.

approach of this type was by Hansen and Nilsson (1960). They found some tendency for average credit periods to lengthen, as regards both exports and imports, in the late 1950s, particularly in the recession year of 1958. It was not clear whether this was the result of more intense competition due to the recession, or part of a trend.

The evidence that there has in fact been such a trend is not very compelling. It is certainly not evident in the British data shown in Table 2.7, which show a breakdown of export credits by the term of payment (concept *A* of Chapter 1).

Results presented by Van Nieuwkerk are also inconsistent with the hypothesis that there has been a general lengthening in credit terms. He used data on the stock of foreign trade credit received by or granted to manufacturing firms with more than 100 employees (which covers about 75% of total Dutch manufacturing), and compared these with estimates of exports and imports of the corresponding sector. While buyer credit received from foreign countries on Dutch exports showed a steady rise, from an average of under 10 days in 1965 to almost 20 days in 1971, none of the other three series showed a secular increase: buyer credit granted to foreign countries was stagnant at a negligible level, while

Table 2.7. *Terms of payment for UK exports* 1967–75

(*Percentages*)

	1967	1969	1971	1973	1975	1975 (our results)
Cash or up to 60 days	56.6	57.5	55.7	56.4	58.1	69.2
61 to 180 days	31.2	31.0	32.4	33.5	32.5	28.0
181 days to 1 yr.	5.5	4.6	4.9	3.8	3.0	1.8
1 yr. to 21 mths } 21 mths to 5 yrs	3.9	3.8	1.1	1.9	1.4	0.0
			2.7	1.9	2.0	1.1
Over 5 years	2.8	3.1	3.2	2.5	3.0	0.0

Source: Board of Trade Journal, Trade and Industry, 1969–77, for first five columns; Questionnaire survey for final column

Table 2.8. *Average terms of payment and credit periods in Sweden and Britain (days)*

	Exports		Imports	
	Sweden 1968	UK 1975	Sweden 1968	UK 1975
Average term of payment (concept A)	78	63	65	42
Average credit period (concept D)	91	82	45	38

Source: Sweden: Grassman (1973a, Table 3.2, p. 42); UK: Questionnaire survey

supplier credits granted (average nearly 40 days) and received (average almost 25 days) both rose and then fell.[3]

Grassman (1973a) derived a more detailed, but snapshot, view of periods of credit in Sweden in 1968 from the Customs Survey. His aggregate results may be summarised by one table and one diagram reproduced from his book. We add our summary results to his table for purposes of comparison and two histograms summarising the distributions of terms of payment found in our samples.

Grassman also disaggregated terms of payment by commodities, the geographical location of the trading partner, and the size of transaction. The longest terms of payment occurred in the shipbuilding industry; indeed, this accounts for much of the long tail in the distribution shown in Figure 2.1. Electrical equipment (on the export side) and cars (on the import side) also had markedly above-average terms of payment, while food (on both sides) and timber (on the export side) were particularly short. Credits tended to be very short in trade with Eastern Europe,

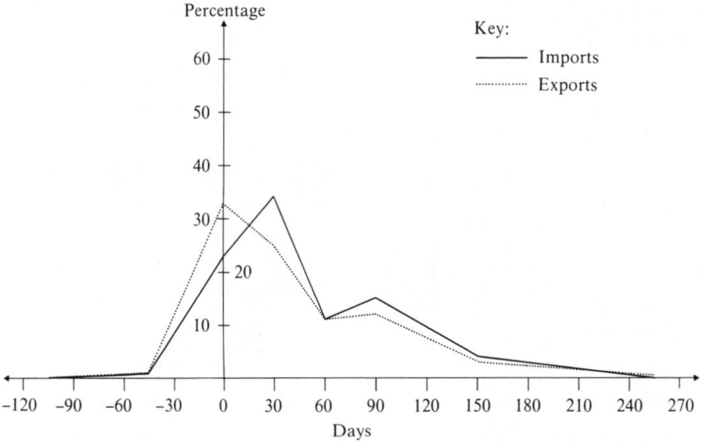

Figure 2.1 Relative frequencies of terms of payment in Swedish foreign trade 1968
Source: Grassman (1973a, Fig. 6.2, p. 120)

Africa and Asia, and particularly long in the case of exports to Latin America and imports from Britain (which may have been due to speculation, given that most imports from Britain were denominated in sterling and that the data were drawn from 1968). Larger transactions tended to involve longer credits.

The results of two other enquiries are consistent with Grassman's findings on differences between commodities. Hansen and Nilsson (1960) found particularly long terms of payment on engineering products and particularly short terms on forest products. The Department of Trade enquiries have found UK export credits to be shortest in the food, drink and tobacco category (over three quarters of exports sold on terms of 60 days or less), and the longest in metal manufacturing, engineering and shipbuilding (the only industries where credits of over a year are significant).[4]

In themselves data on the stock of outstanding trade credit and the length of periods of credit reveal very little about the implications of trade credit practices for balance of payments developments. They enable one to make some estimate of the impact of a change in trade (measured on a transactions basis) for the balance of payments, but that is about all. For example, if one can assume that the distribution of credit periods is similar to that of terms of payment, then data such as those depicted in

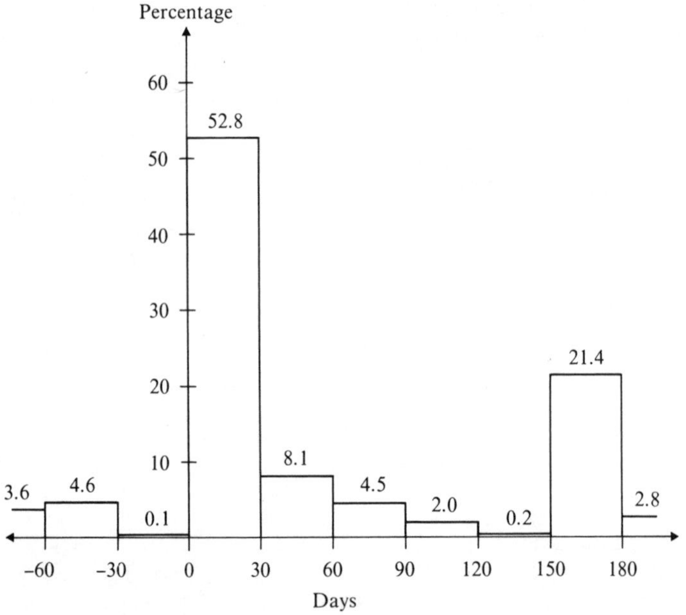

Figure 2.2 Relative frequencies of terms of payment in British exports 1975
Source: Questionnaire survey

Figure 2.2 enable one to estimate the time profile of the payments impact of an across-the-board rise in exports. Some receipts start to accrue even before the exports are made; this stream builds up rapidly to a peak in the month the exports are made; it then declines quite rapidly in the British case, but with some receipts still accruing several years later. This explains why increased exports tend to lead to an outflow of capital (as they have been found to do in econometric studies), and hence why an improvement in the balance of trade does not normally lead to an equal improvement in the overall balance of payments. But these data do not reveal the potential variability of trade credits, i.e. the scope for leading and lagging, and it is this variability that has really important implications for economic management. This variability depends on the elasticity of the period of credit.

Very little indeed is known on this topic, despite its importance. The Committee on the Working of the Monetary System (Radcliffe Report, 1959, paras. 639–40) asserted that it was impossible to measure the maximum reserve loss that could result from leads and lags, but that it could run into hundreds of millions of pounds without infringing existing regulations and that it had in fact approached £100 millions in the third quarter of 1957 (when exports averaged about £280 millions per month). Hansen and Nilsson (1960) found that credit terms could vary sub-

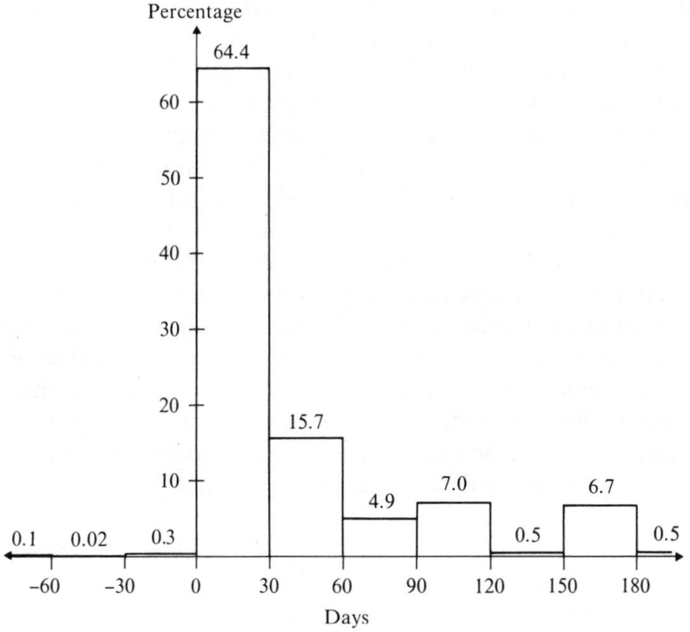

Figure 2.3 Relative frequencies of terms of payment in British imports 1975
Source: Questionnaire survey

stantially within a year, and ascribed the variations they observed primarily to changes in domestic and foreign monetary conditions. Van Nieuwkerk (1979) also found significant year to year variations in credit periods in Dutch trade. Einzig (1962, 1968) wrote at length about the different channels through which firms can engage in leading and lagging, but the only figures cited were the not very relevant ones of stocks of outstanding credits. Uggla (1970) gave some estimates of the funds susceptible to leading and lagging in Swedish trade in 1968, but since these figures did not distinguish between open account and other methods of settlement, and did not include any estimate of the length of time for which export receipts might be lagged, the figures quoted do not provide an estimate of the potential drain on the reserves. Grassman (1973a) showed that open-account transactions, which are by far the most elastic,[5] were of dominant importance in Swedish trade. That seems to be about all that the literature has to offer. We endeavour to do something to improve on this state of affairs in Chapter 6.

At one time there was some tendency to assume that variations in trade credit were virtually synonymous with the balance of payments residual, in which case an econometric explanation of the latter could be regarded as a way of throwing light on the former. However, most of those who have examined the question, such as Hansen and Nilsson (1960), Grassman (1967), and Einzig (1968, Appendix), have concluded that there are too many other items included in the residual (smuggling, misinvoicing, translation of foreign-currency-invoiced items covered forward into domestic currency at the spot rate prevailing on the date t_E or t_I rather than at the forward rate prevailing on t_F,[6] unrecorded capital flows, sampling errors in estimates of tourist expenditures, etc.) to permit one to rely on measuring leading and lagging this way. This conclusion was also argued in Hansen (1961), a mainly theoretical work. The main dissent from this view is in an early paper by Katz (1953), and he qualified his dissent very substantially. In addition Einzig classifies variations in the timing of actual exports and imports and in the forward covering of trade transactions as forms of leading and lagging, and therefore regards the residual as not only including a number of items other than leading and lagging but also as excluding some forms of the phenomena. Our own definition is restricted to variations in the timing of payments, but even so the arguments against indirect measurement of leads and lags by the balance of payments residual seem compelling.

3

DATA COLLECTION

In this chapter we describe the methods by which our data were collected, explain the purposes of the questions posed in our questionnaires, provide more technical and comprehensive explanations of the different methods of settlement, and give some details of our samples. We also report on the results of some interviews with bankers conducted in the early stage of our study, and on a second set of interviews with a few of the firms that responded to our questionnaire, which were conducted later on.

When Grassman (1973a) conducted his study of financing practices in Swedish foreign trade, he was able to analyse a random sample of about 10,000 transactions. This survey was undertaken by the Swedish customs authorities, and firms were legally obliged to respond to the questionnaires they received. Similarly, his later study (1976) was based on a properly constructed stratified sample of 3,656 transactions out of the 5.2 millions registered with the Swedish customs in 1973, and virtually all recipients responded as they were legally obliged to do.

We knew from the start, of course, that we would not have the help of legal compulsion in obtaining a high response rate, but that we would have to rely on the goodwill of British business. We did, however, hope to be able to construct a random sample of British trade transactions over our chosen data period. Since all British trade is registered with HM Customs, we approached them for help. Unfortunately for us, they eventually decided that to release even a random sample of firms' names and addresses together with registration numbers identifying a transaction would be a breach of the confidential basis on which firms had supplied information to them. We were therefore compelled to circulate our questionnaires, not to a random sample as we had hoped, but to a group of trading firms that were as representative as we could achieve in the circumstances. How these firms were chosen is described in Section 3.4; how they were asked to select a transaction is described at the end of Section 3.1; and some assessment of the sample thus obtained is contained in Section 3.5.

3.1 The questionnaires

As described in the Introduction, we embarked on this study with the aims of shedding light on such matters as the short-run behaviour of exchange markets, leads and lags, the use of forward markets, and the factors that influenced decisions on trade financing practices. This largely determined the subjects our questionnaires had to explore. The export and import questionnaires were deliberately made as similar as possible, with the aim of making our results on the two sides of the trade accounts comparable. The export questionnaire is reproduced on pp. 37–39, and the import questionnaire on pp. 39–41.

The first point to note is that we asked that data relate to an invoice from an individual transaction. There were two reasons for asking about an individual transaction. The first was to ensure that we received precise answers rather than general opinions; that we were told about what had been done, albeit on only one occasion, rather than being given the respondent's views either on what ought to be done, or what he thought we would expect to hear. The second aim was to make the sample as close to a random sample as was possible: firms were in fact asked to give us details of the first transaction they came across in their records of the stipulated time period.

The time period was chosen by two criteria. It had to be fairly recent, both so that firms could find it easily and so that it provided information on present-day practices, but it had to be sufficiently far in the past to ensure that most transactions had been settled. We also wanted it to be in a period when exchange markets were reasonably tranquil, so that, if something called normal behaviour did exist, we would observe it. These considerations led us to February 1975. (The export questionnaire, the first to be sent out, was circulated in June 1976. The import questionnaire was sent out later, but for comparability we asked for information from the same period as for the export questionnaire.)

3.2 The meaning and purpose of the questions

The present section seeks to explain the purpose of each question that we asked. Comments refer to both the export and the import questionnaire. As some of the terms in use in trade financing are restricted to that area, we provide a glossary of these terms describing methods of settlement.

The purpose of questions 2–4 in Section A is almost self-evident. It is to reveal the influence, on the practices to be elicited in the following questions, of the type of goods involved, the country of the trading partner, and whether the trading partners were independent firms or constituents of the same MNC.

A study of the financing of UK exports

This questionnaire relates to an invoice concerning an export transaction. The invoice should be the first to be conveniently located from amongst such invoices dated *February* 1975. If there are not any export invoices for this month then select the first one thereafter.

Where alternative responses are provided please tick as appropriate.

Section A

1. Name of Company ____________________
2. What was the commodity, or SITC number of the commodity exported in this transaction? ____________________
3. To which country were the goods exported (i.e. country of buyer)? ____________________
4. Are you affiliated to the buyer in this transaction (e.g. as parent or subsidiary company)?

   Yes ☐ No ☐

Section B

1. Date of invoice / / 1975
2. What were the terms of payment stipulated in the contract covered by the invoice:

a) open account	☐	____ days from ________ (date)
open account (periodic settlements)	☐	settlement every ____ month(s)
b) cash on delivery of goods	☐	
c) cash against documents	☐	
d) acceptance of bills against documents	☐	due within ____ days from ____ (date)
e) payment of bills against documents	☐	
f) time documentary credit (acceptance credit)	☐	due within ____ days from ____ (date)
g) sight documentary credit (letter of credit)	☐	
h) advance (full amount)	☐	
i) consignment	☐	
j) instalments	☐	Terms: ____________
k) other	☐	Terms: ____________

3. If not already indicated above, what was the latest date of payment allowed to the buyer? ____________________
4. Was cash discount offered for early payment?

   Yes ☐ No ☐

5. Did the contract allow for deferred payment subject to an interest charge or other penalty?

   Yes ☐ No ☐

6. In which currency was the sale invoiced:
   a) sterling ☐
   b) that of the country of the buyer ☐
   c) that of a third country ☐ ____ (currency used)
7. What was the value of the sale, expressed in the currency of invoice.

   ____

8. Has payment by the buyer been in accordance with the terms given above?

   Yes ☐ No ☐ Payment not yet due ☐

9. What were the dates of the following procedures concerning the goods covered by the invoice:
   a) placement of order ____________
   b) clearance by HM Customs ____________
   c) delivery to the buyer ____________
   d) payment(s) by the buyer ____________

Section C

1. Is there a specialist department, or group of staff, advising on foreign exchange matters within your company?

   Yes ☐ No ☐

2. Did you use the forward exchange market in connection with this transaction?

   Yes ☐ No ☐

   Do you generally use the forward exchange market in connection with your exporting?

   Yes ☐ No ☐

3. Did you cover or reduce the foreign exchange risk involving this transaction in any other way (e.g. by borrowing or 'matching')?

   Yes ☐ No ☐

4. Were any ECGD facilities used to help finance this transaction?

   Yes ☐ No ☐

5. Were any provisions made in the contract concerning this transaction guarding against changes in production or trading conditions (e.g. as cost escalation clauses or stipulations relating to price variations resulting from changes in exchange rates)?

   Yes ☐ No ☐

   If 'yes' briefly specify the nature of these provisions:

   ____

   ____

   ____

Section D

1. Approximately how long has your company been involved in exporting?

   Under 2 years ☐ 2 to 5 years ☐ over 5 years ☐

2. Approximately how long has your company been exporting to this buyer?

   Under 2 years ☐ 2 to 5 years ☐ over 5 years ☐

3. Do you regularly sell to this buyer?

   Yes ☐ No ☐

4. For the financial year ending in 1975, could you state the approximate value of:
   a) total company turnover ____________
   b) total company exports ____________
   c) exports of this particular commodity ____________

5. Does your company import directly from overseas?

   Yes ☐ No ☐

   If 'yes', would you be willing to complete a questionnaire of very similar character to this, relating to an import purchase transaction?

   Yes ☐ No ☐

Section E

We would greatly appreciate any further information that you feel is not covered by this questionnaire but which is relevant to your replies, along with any views and comments you wish to make. It would be particularly helpful if you could indicate whether the details given regarding the currency of invoice and terms of payment used in this transaction are representative of your usual transactions involving the commodity and trading partner in question.

____

____

____

____

____

____

____

____

____

Name:________ Position within Company: ____________

Please contact Stephen Carse at the Department of Economics, University of Warwick, if you require any assistance in completing the questionnaire, or desire further information concerning the aims and purpose of the research programme.

A study of the financing of UK imports

This questionnaire relates to an invoice concerning a direct import purchase. The invoice should be the first to be conveniently located from amongst such invoices dated February 1975, or dated as close to this period as possible.

Where alternative responses are provided please tick as appropriate.

Section A

1. Name of your Company ____________
2. What was the commodity imported in this transaction? ____________
2. From which country were the goods imported (i.e. country of seller)? ____________

   ____
4. Are you affiliated to the seller in this transaction (e.g. as parent or subsidiary company)?

   Yes ☐ No ☐

Section B

1. Date of invoice / /1975
2. What were the terms of payment stipulated in the contract covered by the invoice:
   - a) open account ☐ ____ days from __________ (date)
     open account (periodic settlements) ☐ settlement every ____ month(s)
   - b) cash on delivery of goods ☐
   - c) cash against documents ☐
   - d) acceptance of bills against documents ☐ due within ____ days from____ (date)
   - e) payment of bills against documents ☐
   - f) time documentary credit (acceptance credit) ☐ due within ____ days from____ (date)
   - g) sight documentary credit (letter of credit) ☐
   - h) advance (full amount) ☐
   - i) consignment ☐
   - j) instalments ☐ Terms: ______________
     ____
   - k) other ☐ Terms: ______________
     ____
3. If not already indicated above, what was the latest permitted date for payment? ____
4. Was cash discount offered for early payment?

   Yes ☐ No ☐
5. Did the contract allow for deferred payment subject to an interest charge or other penalty?

   Yes ☐ No ☐
6. In which currency was the purchase invoiced:
   - a) sterling ☐
   - b) that of the country of the seller ☐
   - c) that of a third country ☐ __________ (currency used)
7. What was the value of the goods purchased, expressed in the currency of invoice?____
8. Has your payment been in accordance with the terms given above?

   Yes ☐ No ☐ Payment not yet due ☐
9. What were the dates of the following procedures concerning the goods covered by the invoice:
   - a) placement of order______________________________
   - b) clearance by HM Customs ______________________________
   - c) delivery by the seller ______________________________
   - d) payment(s) to the seller ______________________________

Section C

1. Is there a specialist department, or group of staff, advising on foreign exchange matters within your company?

   Yes ☐ No ☐

2. Did you use the forward exchange market in connection with this transaction?

   Yes ☐ No ☐

   Did you generally use the forward exchange market in connection with your importing at the time of this transaction?

   Yes ☐ No ☐

3. Did you cover or reduce the foreign exchange risk involving this transaction in any other way (e.g. by borrowing or 'matching')?

   Yes ☐ No ☐

4. Were any provisions made in the contract concerning this transaction guarding against changes in production or trading conditions (e.g. as cost escalation clauses or stipulations relating to price variations resulting from changes in exchange rates)?

   Yes ☐ No ☐

   If 'yes' briefly specify the nature of these provisions:

   ____

   ____

Section D

1. Approximately how long has your company been involved in importing?

   Under 2 years ☐ 2 to 5 years ☐ over 5 years ☐

2. Approximately how long has your company been importing from this seller?

   Under 2 years ☐ 2 to 5 years ☐ over 5 years ☐

3. Do you regularly purchase from this seller?

   Yes ☐ No ☐

4. For the financial year ending in 1975, could you state the approximate value of:
   a) total company turnover ______________________________
   b) total company imports ______________________________
   c) imports of this particular commodity ______________________________

Section E

We would greatly appreciate any further information that you feel is not covered by this questionnaire but which is relevant to your replies, along with any views and comments you wish to make. It would be particularly helpful if you could indicate whether the details given regarding the currency of invoice and terms of payment used in this transaction are representative of your usual transactions involving the commodity and trading partner in question.

____

____

____

____

____

Name: __________ Position within Company: ______________________________

Please contact Stephen Carse at the Department of Economics, University of Warwick if you require any assistance in completing the questionnaire, or desire further information concerning the aims and purpose of the research programme.

Section B, questions 2–5, relate to the method of settlement, the terms of payment, and the elasticity of the period of credit. Question 2 asked for the method of settlement and the term of payment, including dates t_A and t_B except where these are implied by the answers to question 9 (of Section B). A classification of methods of settlement was provided in Chapter 1; we include here a more detailed and comprehensive glossary explaining the terms that appear in question 2.[1]

Glossary

(a) *Open account.* The distinguishing feature is that no legal documentation or bills of exchange are used, payment being made simply in response to presentation of an invoice. This is the most flexible form of settlement, involving the least administrative burden and the greatest variability in the period of credit taken. There are two variants of this method:
   (i) goods are despatched by the exporter with the requirement that payment be remitted within an agreed period;
   (ii) goods are despatched by the exporter on the basis of an arrangement that settlement will be made on a regular basis, e.g. on the last day of each month. (This procedure may be used when there are regular transactions between the trading partners.)

(b) *Cash on delivery.* Strictly speaking, this means that the goods are not handed over to the buyer until payment has been received. However, it is a well-established practice in some trades for the seller to hand over the goods a few days before receiving payment, to allow the buyer time to inspect what he has bought. Even then, however, there is very little flexibility in the period of credit once the goods have been despatched; payment can be led or lagged only by leading or lagging shipment.

(c) *Cash against documents.* When this case is strictly interpreted, documents of entitlement are not handed over until payment is received. It is therefore very similar to cash on delivery in terms of its economic effects; payment can be lagged only by foregoing receipt of the goods, and that cannot usually be delayed for long, if at all. This method does, however, sometimes allow more scope for *leading* of payments, e.g. when transport time is uncertain and the seller simply specifies a final date for payment.

(d) *Acceptance of bills against documents.* Under this method, documents of entitlement are given to the buyer when he accepts a bill of exchange drawn up for a fixed term (and therefore known as a usance, tenor, or term bill). Once the buyer has accepted a bill, he has to settle it on maturity, and to prevent him lengthening the period of credit by delaying acceptance, the seller frequently specifies the date of acceptance, e.g. on sight of goods or documents. This method therefore results in a very inflexible maximum to the period of credit, but not necessarily in a short period. Bills can, however, be settled before they mature. In some Far East countries, indeed, documents are not allowed (by law) to be handed over until payment has been made even though the exporter has allowed this method of settlement, and in the UK discounts are sometimes offered for early settlement; in such cases bills may well be settled before they have matured.

(e) *Payment of bills against documents.* This method is rather similar to cash against documents in many respects: indeed, some of our respondents did not distinguish between the two methods. The difference is that a bill of exchange is used to effect payment – in this case a sight or demand bill. The exporter receives payment immediately upon presentation of the bill together with the necessary documents establishing delivery, whereupon the documents of entitlement are released to the buyer.[2] This procedure normally allows no scope for leading or lagging.

(f) *Time documentary credit.* Documentary credits provide the most binding method of settlement. The procedure is that the importer makes arrangements for the exporter to draw bills on his account via a bank in the exporter's own country. The bills can be drawn without recourse to the importer, provided that the stipulated documents have been received by the importer's correspondent bank in the exporter's country. The bills drawn under a time documentary credit are for a particular maturity, hence the name 'time' (or 'term' or 'acceptance') credit. As with acceptance of bills against documents, this technique permits a significant length of credit but little flexibility. Indeed, it allows none at all to the importer, since the bills are drawn by the exporter at his discretion subject to the availability of the documents, and it is the availability of these which, in turn, allows the importer to take delivery of the goods.

(g) *Sight documentary credit.* Under this arrangement the bills drawn by the exporter are not for a fixed term but are sight or demand bills, i.e. bills that will be paid immediately by the importer's bank provided that they are accompanied by the proper documentation providing proof of shipment. (The modern tendency is for bills not to be used, but for the documents themselves to be presented to the bank instead, i.e. to use cash against documents instead of sight documentary credits.) This arrangement allows very little in the way of length or flexibility of the period of credit, especially to the importer.

(h) *Advance.* Payment in advance of receipt of goods, while possible in principle, appears to be rare in practice, except for part advance payments for contracts involving payment by instalments.

(i) *Consignment.* In this case the buyer pays when he has sold the goods, rather than when he receives them. (Grassman treats this as a special form of open account; we discuss the appropriateness of this classification in Chapter 5, pp. 84).

(j) *Instalments.* Payment by instalments is usually found only on very large transactions involving the purchase of capital goods. It is common in such cases for an advance payment to be made for a part of the cost. The instalments may be paid by the use of term bills.

Question 3 was intended to capture any restriction on settlement date t_B not implied by the answer to (2), while questions 4 and 5 looked for any incentives, other than expected exchange rate changes, to vary the timing of payments.

Question 6, on currency of invoicing, was phrased so as to elicit information on whether the exporter's, the importer's, or a vehicle currency was used. Questions 7, 8 and 9 each relate to quite different purposes, and were placed at that point simply because they were, with one possible exception, the last questions which could be answered by reference to the invoice. Question 7 was needed to let us know what proportion (by value) of UK trade we eventually had information on and would also reveal any systematic influence of size of transaction; question 8 was primarily designed to let us know whether the formal answers to question 2 approximated to what was actually done, and (9) let us locate temporally the various stages of the transaction about its appearance in the trade figures (i.e. to relate t_0, t_D and t_P to t_E or t_I).

Section C looks at more general matters, on which we did not expect most invoices to carry information. Question 1 is an attempt to gauge the importance attached to trade financing practices by companies, while questions 2–4 sought information on the extent to which firms used methods, including use of the forward market, which could insulate them from the effects of fluctuating exchange rates.[3]

Section D provides information on trading experience, and on the importance of foreign trade for the company. Section E elicited a range of comments, mainly on how the respondents' behaviour had altered since 1975. These are introduced as appropriate in the following chapters.

3.3 Trial and error process

The questionnaires as shown of course represent their final form; there were several preliminary versions. These were discussed initially with members of both the CBI and HM Treasury, and, after noting and taking account of their comments, a pilot survey was carried out.

Although the main purpose of this was to ensure that there were no ambiguities or major omissions in our questionnaire, it did of course yield results. These were reported in an article by Wood and Carse (1976). Although the sample was very small, most of the results were to prove strikingly close to those we obtained from our full sample. It was also useful in further 'de-bugging' the questionnaire. Three changes are worth noting. First, the list of possible credit arrangements (Section B, question 2) is not exhaustive; we eliminated some which appear to exist in principle but were not used in practice.[4] Second, notable as a curiosity, is that our original wording asked for information from a 'specific invoice' – by which we meant an invoice relating to one specific transaction. That wording had to be changed to the form shown when it was discovered that a 'specific invoice' was actually a particular kind of unusually detailed invoice which was now dying out and which had been used primarily in trade with the USA. Third, we added the request for the 'date of order' in order to provide more information on the time lags involved in trade.

3.4 The choice of sample

3.4.1 *Exports*

The major source of exporting firms was the Extel Statistical Service British Company and Unquoted British Companies Annual Cards. These provide information on most UK companies, and on all with a stock exchange quotation. Since private unquoted companies are practically completely confined to small firms, this ensured that we contacted almost all companies with exports of over £3m p.a. in 1974 and most with exports of £1 m. p.a. to £2 m. p.a. in that year, and gave us a choice of firms with exports down to as little as £1,000 p.a. We also, to ensure adequate representation of large companies, chose a further hundred from Dun and Bradstreet's *Guide to Key British Enterprises* (1975/76 edition).

We contacted all the main UK exporting groups, and a random sample of smaller exporters. Also, we weighted our sample by sending two questionnaires (so as to receive information on two transactions) to all companies whose (visible) exports exceeded £2m in their financial year ended 1974. (This was just over 25% of the exporting firms we contacted.)

In total, we sent questionnaires to 2,400 exporting companies. We received a response of some sort from 1,443; of these 982 (41%) completed questionnaires, returning altogether 1,252 questionnaires. These covered just over 1% by value of a month's visible exports at the time to which our sample relates.

3.4.2 *Imports*

Again we used the Extel Statistical Service Cards, and also sent import questionnaires to all those exporting firms who had indicated both that they also imported and that they were willing to give further assistance. The major source of importers, however, was the *Directory of British Importers* (1975).

In total we contacted 2,000 importing firms, sending two questionnaires to firms we knew had imports over £2 millions, and received 901 completed questionnaires from 810 firms. This was a response rate of 40.5%. The transactions covered represented 0.7% of the value of monthly British imports in the first half of 1975. Both of these respectable but not overwhelming response rates were attained after sending out a follow-up letter.

3.5 Representativeness of the samples

A random sample of around 1,000 can normally be relied on to provide results of a useful degree of accuracy. Unfortunately, for reasons described at the beginning of this chapter, we were not able to draw on a random sample. There is no way of establishing conclusively whether, or what sort of, biases will have been introduced into our samples as a result. There is, however, one straightforward way of checking whether our samples appear representative of UK trade as a whole, and that is to compare their commodity breakdowns with those shown in the trade statistics for British exports and imports. This is done in Table 3.1 (excluding SITC 9).

Our disaggregation was largely at the SITC 1-digit level. However, we formed a special category of 'large bulky capital goods' (e.g. ships, electrical generators, complete process plants) drawn from parts of SITC 7 in order to treat separately those goods where credit terms could be expected to be an important competitive factor, and therefore especially long. We also treated SITC 67–68, which consist of the homogeneous semi-processed metals, separately from the rest of SITC 6, since their homogeneity makes it likely that, unlike other manufactured goods, their prices will be effectively determined by demand and supply in worldwide markets and hence implies that they should be classified as tradables II rather than tradables I. We assumed that all other manufactured goods (SITC 5–8) were tradables I, and we treated the whole of SITC 0–4 (as well as 67–68) as tradables II. This classification is certainly far from perfect; Scotch whisky, for example, is surely a differentiated product with an administered price and would therefore be better placed in the tradable I category; more generally one may suspect that the UK has very few genuine tradable II exports. Nevertheless, we judged that tests conducted on this objective basis would be more convincing than ones where we assigned each sampled product to one or other category *ad hoc*, since such a procedure can lay one open to the suspicion that products may have been assigned to categories on the basis of the financing procedures observed, thereby biasing and invalidating the test procedure. Table 3.1 shows, among the memorandum items, the breakdown between tradables I and II.

It is apparent from Table 3.1 that, on the export side, SITC 7 is over-represented and all other categories, except fuels, are under-represented in our sample as compared to the whole of UK exports. The biggest discrepancy on the import side is the over-representation of chemicals in the sample. Nevertheless, we do not feel that the discrepancies are so marked as to justify serious concern.

Table 3.1. *Comparison of commodity composition of our samples with UK exports and imports in* 1975

(*Percentages by value*)

		Exports		Imports	
		Sample	Trade	Sample	Trade
Commodity group					
SITC	*Products*				
0–1	Food, drink & tobacco	5.7	7.4	23.1	18.6
2	Crude materials	2.1	2.8	12.3	8.8
3	Fuels & oils	4.2	4.2	15.3	18.4
4	Animal/vegetable oils & fat	negligible	0.1	0.8	0.7
5	Chemicals	7.3	11.4	15.4	6.0
60–66 69	Manufactures classified by materials	10.9	15.9	13.0	13.2
67–68	Iron & steel & non-ferrous metals	3.6	6.3	3.8	7.0
71–72	Electrical & other machinery	35.2	30.0	9.3	14.3
73	Vehicles and parts	3.0	12.7	1.6	5.0
8	Miscellaneous manufactures	3.7	9.2	5.5	8.0
Part of 7	Large bulky capital goods	24.3	n.a.	0.0	n.a.
		100	100	100	100
Memorandum items					
7	Vehicles & parts, electrical & other machinery	62.5	42.7	10.9	19.3
0–4 67–68	Tradables II	15.6	20.8	55.3	53.5
5–8 exc. 67–68	Tradables I	84.4	79.2	44.8	46.5

Source: Monthly Digest of Statistics, July 1976, and questionnaire survey

3.6 Interviews with bankers

We supplemented the data drawn from our questionnaire survey by two sets of interviews. The first series was with bankers, and was conducted early in our investigation, before we had received many responses to our questionnaires. The second series was conducted, after all our questionnaires were in, with some of the firms that had completed questionnaires. We report first on the results of our interviews with bankers.

These interviews with bankers were conducted with the aim of finding out:

(a) what sort of advice firms were generally given by their bankers
(b) what channels connected the banks with clients seeking advice on foreign currency matters;
(c) what bankers thought their clients generally did, with regard to currency of invoicing, forward covering, and granting or receiving credit.

We interviewed bankers at the London Clearing Banks, and at foreign banks which had UK offices. These two groups proved to be sharply different in their respective attitudes towards trade financing. (That is of course certainly not to imply that views *within* the groups were identical.)

3.6.1 *The London clearing banks*

All these banks expected a firm's initial approach for advice to be via the manager of the branch where the firm had its account(s). This branch manager could then either himself refer to a specialist section at head office for advice, or put his clients in direct contact with that specialist section. The banks had fairly different attitudes towards non-customers seeking advice. One bank, for example, would be 'reluctant to spend much time' advising a non-client, while another was quite happy to advise non-clients, in the hope of turning them into clients. A third was just about to start a compaign of actively attracting new custom; it had been prompted to do this by an 'upsurge' of custom being attracted away by banks at the foreign end of the transaction.

As to who sought advice, there was agreement that firms habitually engaged in foreign trade generally had a department – albeit often a small one – dealing with trade financing. Almost no firm, except for those just starting to trade abroad, relied continually on their bank for advice. Firms, rather, were said to turn to banks for advice on problems their own advisers had not encountered before.

This passivity of the banks was perhaps surprising, in view of their fairly widely-held belief that UK firms tend to be somewhat casual in their trade financing arrangements. An example we were given of this was of a UK firm which sent abroad its senior engineers to assess the costs of carrying out a long-term capital project. These engineers were also expected to arrange the financing.

In view of this belief that UK firms were not very skilled at managing their trade financing, it was not surprising that the clearing banks all advised their clients always to cover forward any exposed foreign exchange position, and to use one of the formal documents which could secure settlement of debts on a precise date.[5] Firms, it was thought, should not 'get involved in currency speculation'. Of course, if a UK firm invoices, or is invoiced in, sterling, then it is free of exchange risk. One of the clearing banks was particularly keen on advising sterling invoicing to its clients, and indeed appeared to view anything else as somewhat unpatriotic. On currency of invoicing, it was generally argued that the buyer usually chose the currency, at any rate at a time of world recession such as when the interviews were conducted. It was also recognised that sterling invoicing was common in UK export trade. The consistency of these beliefs is not self-evident.

As to the method of settlement, bills of exchange were generally recommended. The banks would encourage open account only when there was a regular flow of trade with a trading partner, or when the trading partner was a large and well-known company. It was conjectured by one bank that, for the latter reason, trade on open account was important in trade with the USA. The bankers all believed that their clients generally took their advice.

3.6.2 *Foreign banks in the UK*

These were somewhat different from the London Clearing Banks in that the banks themselves seemed to be more active, and gave less 'cautious' advice to their clients. In particular, all these banks saw their knowledge of foreign currencies and foreign economies as their major competitive weapon in gaining business. They went out and volunteered advice, as a way of winning business. One had representatives who visited firms, while another organised regular regional 'seminars', to which both clients and non-clients were invited.

But, despite this, their clients were in general experienced foreign traders, who had often first come into contact with the banks in the banks' home countries. The banks themselves suggested that the fact that they dealt with experienced firms influenced the advice they gave.

They did not press sterling invoicing on clients, nor did they advise complete forward cover of any foreign exchange exposure. This arose partly from the knowledge that they were dealing with firms which habitually took a view about likely future exchange rate movements, and which were aware of the extra costs involved in using the forward market. But one had recognised a point which we noted in Chapter 1 – that holding a stock of imports (at least of tradables II) can itself be protection against currency risk.

Unlike the London Clearing Banks, they thought that the predominant means of settlement was on open account. This of course may well be due to their dealing particularly with traders for whom the London Clearing Banks thought open account was most suitable – experienced traders – and may reflect the bias of several of these bankers towards trade with the USA. This difference, in other words, may arise not from different attitudes, but rather from dealing with a special class of customer. The current predominance of open account was thought by one long-established foreign bank to be the outcome of a trend that had been discernible since the mid 1950s. This had been a trend away from documentary credits, initially towards bills of exchange, and now to the least formal terms of all. This trend was thought to have been at least in part due to a general increase in trust and confidence between traders. The bankers were of the opinion that there had not been any significant move toward *longer* credits.

Several of these bankers thought that the US dollar was a dominant 'vehicle' currency. This may, of course, in part reflect their US connection.

In summary, the general picture of financing practices which emerged from meetings with these foreign banks was markedly different from the general picture which emerged at the London Clearing Banks. The difference was mainly one of attitude – the banks were more active in seeking business, and their clients more active in foreign exchange management. Probably for this reason, it was only from these banks that we encountered complaints about the restrictiveness of UK exchange controls. These banks were also involved with the trade financing practices of their clients on a much more regular and continuing basis than were the London Clearing Banks; this was, they thought, because of their clients' fairly frequent foreign exchange exposure.

3.7 Interviews with firms

Our second set of interviews, with a few of the companies that had responded, focussed particularly on amplifying the comments that these companies had added to the questionnaire. Twenty-four firms were interviewed. Of these, fifteen were both exporters and importers, five were solely exporters and four solely importers. They ranged in size from a company with an annual turnover of just on £2 m. to two of the UK's largest companies. The responses to our questions are discussed, under various headings, below. The interviews were carried out in the second half of 1977.

Currency of invoice There was almost unanimous agreement that the exporter could choose the currency of invoice, and that his choice was generally accepted by the buyer. Several firms did, however, comment that buyers were insisting on influencing the currency of invoice to a much greater extent than in previous years. This, it appears, was particularly the case with buyers from West Germany and the USSR, from both of whom there was a markedly increased desire to be invoiced in sterling. The interviews also confirmed our earlier impression that it was not necessarily the larger companies which were most knowledgeable. Indeed, perhaps because they were smaller, several of the smaller companies displayed great flexibility in tailoring the contract to the desires of the client.

Several practices to avoid exchange risk were, however, restricted by their nature to the larger companies. Most notable was that, in the group which both exported and imported, only the larger companies 'matched' currencies of invoice so as to have as close to zero foreign exchange exposure as they could obtain. We also discovered that, among the larger companies, there was a clear tendency to use foreign currency invoicing – particularly using the US dollar as a third currency – for the larger transactions. The impression was given that only for larger transactions was foreign currency invoicing worth the additional effort.

The principal part of that additional effort, we gathered, was quite frequently overcoming resistance by buyers. Further, every company interviewed was at pains to point out that changing to foreign currency invoicing could not be done lightly because they thought it impractical from both their own and their clients' viewpoints to be changing frequently. Once taken, the decision had to be adhered to, certainly for at least five years or so. Nonetheless, there was a continuing trend (as indicated also by the Department of Trade surveys) towards foreign currency invoicing of exports.

We also found that some of the importers had switched away from asking to be invoiced in sterling. One company said quite explicitly that they had done this because their suppliers increased their prices so much if the goods were invoiced in sterling that they were better off being invoiced in foreign currency, which left them free to choose whether or not to cover on the basis of their view of the outlook for sterling.

Since there had been a clear trend towards foreign currency invoicing, we asked those exporting firms who invoiced in sterling why they did so. The explanations were diverse. Some said it was in response to pressure from buyers, but in more cases it reflected attitudes to, and knowledge about, foreign exchange exposure. Several of these firms said they invoiced in sterling to avoid exchange risk, which as we have argued in Chapter 1 is rational for exporters of tradables I. One had decided that sterling would strengthen in the future, and therefore stayed with sterling to avoid frequent changes in invoicing practices. Another told us that they had invoiced their exports in sterling because most of their business was within the UK, and they did not think it worth while to set up the necessary department to handle foreign currency invoicing. A third remarked that they stayed with sterling to avoid risk because they did not understand the forward market. There was also a firm which said that it was 'not our business to speculate in foreign currencies', and another which said that all their bank accounts were in sterling and that they 'think in terms of sterling, not foreign currencies'.

Before leaving currency of invoice, two other responses are noteworthy. One company told us that they stayed with sterling because its depreciation consistently gave them a competitive edge abroad. The other response was from a firm which had invoiced in foreign currency before a depreciation of sterling, and then, because the customers complained, 'gave them a bit back'. This firm now makes a practice of offering a discount if goods are invoiced in foreign currency and sterling subsequently depreciates. This practice may reflect rational, long-run, profit maximisation, but as the firm had to be nationalised to save it from bankruptcy, one is not sure.

Use of the forward market We found importers markedly more knowledgeable about the forward market than exporters were; this was really to be expected, as the former group had much longer experience of foreign currency invoicing. When we found a company invoicing (or being invoiced) in foreign currency, but not using the forward market, we asked why. Alarmingly, the most frequent response was that no one in the company understood forward covering. Next most common was that the company had decided that, since it was a regular foreign trader, on balance it neither gained nor lost through foreign exchange exposure. Various other reasons were also given; transactions were too small, and the costs exceeded any conceivable gains – these, although given by different companies, are presumably really the same reason. One very interesting response was that, because delivery dates were uncertain, a company had given up using the forward market as it had on occasions incurred substantial costs when rolling over forward contracts. Another firm remarked that using the market imposed 'stricter credit control and financial planning on a company', and that these costs did not justify themselves. A few noted that their spread of currencies was, they thought, sufficiently wide to protect them. One very puzzling explanation for not using the market, given the year of our interviews, was that the exporter used 'hard currencies only'.

Despite the explanations for not using the forward market, however, several firms had started to use it since the year to which our questionnaire related (1975), and most of those which had used it in that year had increased their use of it (as a proportion of their trade) by 1977.

Methods of settlement Without exception all the companies we interviewed were aware of the range of methods of settlement open to them. This was in marked contrast to their knowledge of forward exchange matters, which perhaps reflects both the experience of years of pegged exchange rates and the fact that, insofar as methods of settlement are concerned, foreign trade is very like domestic trade.

The pattern of methods of settlement was really as expected. Simple methods – notably open account – were used with affiliates and partners of long standing, and with trade with EEC countries and the USA. Stricter methods were used with recent trading partners, and with more geographically distant countries. (Several firms mentioned the desirability of using strict methods of settlement when dealing with Latin America.) Transaction size was also said to be an influential factor, while companies without much foreign trading experience generally said they just followed ECGD guidelines.

None of the companies we interviewed had experienced a trend toward looser settlement terms in the 1970s.

Credit terms Neither had any detected any lengthening of credit terms in recent years, whether the companies exported, imported, or did both. Exporters did, however, frequently experience delays in receiving payment. Four main explanations for these delays were given; they are given here in order of frequency. By far the most common was that transit time for the goods was unexpectedly slow; there was an impression that transit times seemed generally to be increasing. Second most frequently given as a cause for late payment were banking delays in transmitting funds. Reasons cited included 'inefficient foreign banking systems' and, from one source, that the 'Chilean government forces delaying of sterling payments'. A few firms said that payment was sometimes delayed by less developed countries experiencing shortages of foreign currency – Nigeria, Sudan, and Zambia were particularly mentioned. Finally, and by far the least important as a cause of late payment, were delays in presenting documents.

Because these causes of delay are largely outside the buyer's control, and also because of the difficulty and cost of enforcement, most companies invoked penalties only against 'flagrant' late payers. Further, most of the larger companies gave very long and flexible credit on small transactions; they regard the cost to their liquidity as negligible in relation to the goodwill, and thereby future orders, generated.

Only one firm in our interview group admitted to using flexible credit terms to lead or lag in any large or regular way. This company, a large one, claimed that it found the practice highly profitable, producing an addition to profit of about £250,000 per month.

Views on banks As firms are inevitably somewhat dependent on the services their banks provide, we sought their views of these services, complementing thereby some of the information we obtained in our interviews with bankers. No clear overall view emerged from the firms we interviewed but, not surprisingly, in view of the gaps some firms readily admitted to exist in their knowledge of trade financing, some strong criticisms were made. These tended to be very general; they can perhaps best be summed up by the remark that the banks 'don't understand an exporter's requirements'. More specifically, criticisms were voiced of a reluctance to extend credit in the light of the bank's own commercial judgment (e.g. one firm complained about 'inflexible overdraft limits'). It also seems clear that some firms, at least, are not well supplied with information by their bankers. One company gave an almost startling example of such bad service. It had several times been quoted incorrect exchange rates by its bankers, and had, in consequence, installed a terminal providing continuous video display of spot and forward exchange rates.

ECGD The work of ECGD is summarised elsewhere (pp. 129–37). Since it was used by a substantial part of our sample (41.4% by value and 21.4% by volume in our questionnaire sample), we sought the views of firms on that organisation. Firms generally praised it but there were two recurrent criticisms.

The first was that there were generally long delays in making decisions involving large transactions with relatively unknown buyers. Second, and clearly a source of irritation, was that the ECGD insisted on including in its comprehensive scheme transactions between branches of an MNC – i.e. that charges were levied for providing cover on riskless transactions.

Decision making We found that responsibility for financing decisions lay sometimes with an accountant, sometimes with a financial director, and, in some cases, with the export sales manager. In large exporting companies, however, two forms of organisation were the rule. Either exports were channelled through a specialist exporting subsidiary, which took financing decisions, or the financing decisions were taken within the finance division at head office, and therefore under the guidance of whoever was in charge of that division. Despite that, when guidelines came from head office, subsidiaries nonetheless frequently saw themselves as final decision makers, with full autonomy to ignore the guidelines. Their decisions would only be questioned should they, as a consequence of losses or illiquidity, need to resort to head office for funds.

In summary, the general impression we received from our interviews was that with the exception of use of the forward market most firms planned their trade financing decisions carefully, but with an eye to the cost of such planning. Our interviews confirmed our hope that one comment which we received on one of our questionnaires was not representative: 'We follow procedures blindly. We don't know how the money comes in, but it does.'

4

INVOICE CURRENCY AND THE USE OF THE FORWARD MARKET

This chapter presents and analyses the results of our enquiries with regard to the first two of the four topics into which we have divided our subject: namely, the currency of invoice and the use of the forward market. In the first section of the chapter we present our results in a series of tables, and note some of the regularities that our data suggest. In the second section we proceed to use the data in order to test the first six of the eight hypotheses developed in Section 1.2.

4.1 The results

Table 4.1 shows the currency of invoice for exports, broken down between sterling (the currency of the exporter), the buyer's currency, the US dollar as a third currency, and other third currencies. Data are presented both for the percentage of the value of exports invoiced in each of these currencies, and the percentage of the number of transactions invoiced in each one. Section A of the table gives the overall result; Section B gives figures broken down by trading partner (the country of the importer); Section C provides a commodity breakdown; Section D disaggregates between transactions between independent firms and intra-MNC transactions (henceforth referred to as disaggregation by affiliation); and Section E provides a breakdown by size of transaction. In each case details of the sample size are provided in the final two columns.

Table 4.2 presents identical data for our sample of import transactions (except, of course, that the trading partners presented in Section B represent the country of the exporter rather than of the importer, and that sterling is the buyer's currency rather than the seller's currency).

Sections A of both tables at first glance seem to provide striking confirmation of the pattern of invoicing first found by Grassman for Sweden and subsequently confirmed in studies of other European countries (see Table 2.1, p. 18–19). That is, invoicing in the exporter's currency is predominant on both sides of the account, followed by the buyer's currency, with the use of a third currency far behind, especially on the export side. Where a third currency is used, however, it is overwhelmingly the US dollar. The other currencies that we found used as third currencies were the Deutsche Mark, Swedish krona, Swiss franc, Dutch guilder and Hong Kong dollar (in both export and import samples); the French franc, yen, and Malawi kwacha (in the export sample only); and the Belgian franc, Danish krone, Canadian dollar, and Chinese rambini (in the import sample only). While most practices conform to expectations, it appears that almost anything is possible on occasion.

Section B of Table 4.1 suggests that the pattern of sterling invoicing of exports predominating is quite general in geographical terms, including the Western hemisphere in general and the USA in particular. Such exceptions there are involve the low share of sterling in invoicing exports to the 'rest of the EEC' and, to a lesser extent, to Japan and Hong Kong, when the measurement is made in terms of the value of exports rather than in terms of the number of transactions. In both of these cases, the result is heavily dependent upon a small number (in fact, respectively three and two) of large foreign currency-invoiced transactions. This may be a problem that is particularly acute because we were not able to draw on a random sample, or it may be that the sample size was simply too small to yield reliable results in value terms given the fact that foreign trade transactions constitute a highly skewed distribution in terms of size of transaction. (Given the erratic fluctuations between successive enquiries of the Department of Trade in the disaggregated results shown in Tables 2.2 and 2.3, pp. 22, 23 we suspect that the latter may be true.) In either event, we concluded that a more reliable picture is probably given by the data for the *number* rather than the *value* of transactions. We continue to present our results on both bases, but in most of what follows we concentrate attention and analysis on the results for the number of transactions. When figures on the value basis have been used in further analysis, as in places in Chapter 6, this is because there are good reasons to believe that behaviour tends to be different for the larger transactions, and it is therefore important that these should be weighted more heavily by using the results by value.

The data on export invoicing to different trading partners by number of transactions show that the use of the buyer's currency is most frequent in trade with the USA, as one would expect, followed by Canada (where the complete absence of invoicing in US dollars in striking), Germany and Switzerland, and the rest of the EEC. The only area where the dollar has a significant vehicle-currency role is in trade with Latin America, and even there it is overwhelmed by sterling invoicing.

Overall, sterling plays a bigger role in the invoicing of British imports than do the buyers' currencies in the invoicing of exports. However, this aggregate result is the consequence of very different patterns found in

Table 4.1. *Currency of invoice, exports*

	Currency of invoice								Sample size	
	Percentage by value				Percentage by number of transactions					
			Third currency				Third currency			
	Pound	Buyer's currency	Dollar	Other	Pound	Buyer's currency	Dollar	Other	Value (£ thousands)	Number of transactions
A *Overall*	75.9	17.3	6.0	0.7	85.5	11.3	2.4	0.8	16,404	1,252
B *By trading partner:*										
Germany & Switzerland	81.8	16.9	1.3	–	69.9	25.8	4.3	–	999	93
Ireland & Channel Islands	100.0	–	–	–	100.0	–	–	–	65	44
Rest of EEC	39.0	51.5	8.9	0.7	77.7	19.6	1.8	0.9	2,877	224
Rest of W. Europe	86.1	11.7	2.0	0.2	85.5	10.8	2.8	0.8	3,605	249
E. Europe and USSR	99.9	–	0.1	–	95.5	–	4.6	–	556	22
Developed Sterling Area	82.1	11.7	5.8	0.3	93.5	4.9	0.8	0.8	502	123
USA	83.4	16.6	n.a.	–	65.2	34.9	n.a.	–	1,267	66
Canada	72.0	28.0	–	–	71.7	28.3	–	–	444	46
Latin America	79.7	–	13.8	6.5	82.2	–	15.6	2.2	1,153	45
Middle East	79.2	8.9	11.9	–	96.8	1.9	1.3	–	3,589	155
Africa, South of Sahara, exc. S. Africa	97.7	–	–	2.3	97.9	–	–	2.1	331	48
Japan and Hong Kong	60.5	24.2	15.3	–	88.0	4.0	4.0	4.0	218	25
Rest of world	98.1	0.1	0.4	1.5	94.6	0.9	2.7	1.8	799	112
C *By commodity:*										
SITC 0–1; Food, drink, tobacco	81.5	16.9	1.0	0.6	83.2	14.0	1.9	0.9	943	107
SITC 2 and 4; Raw materials	48.1	33.7	18.2	–	66.0	26.0	8.0	–	350	50
SITC 3; Fuels & lubricants	99.2	–	0.9	–	84.6	–	15.4	–	683	13
SITC 5; Chemicals	49.3	29.4	20.5	0.6	84.9	9.1	4.5	1.5	1,174	132

SITC 6; Manufactures classified by material	75.6	16.7	4.2	3.5	83.0	14.9	1.3	0.8	2,385	376
SITC 71–2; Machinery & electrical equipment	70.2	19.8	9.9	0.1	89.2	7.1	3.4	0.3	5,777	295
SITC 73; Vehicles exc. ships	92.0	8.0	–	–	93.1	5.6	–	1.4	506	72
SITC 8; Miscellaneous manufactures	84.7	12.3	0.2	2.9	88.7	9.7	0.5	1.1	612	185
Large capital goods	86.0	14.0	–	–	81.8	18.2	–	–	3,975	22
Tradables I	75.7	17.1	6.4	0.8	87.9	9.3	2.0	0.9	13,888	1,025
Tradables II	77.3	18.3	4.2	0.2	74.5	20.7	4.4	0.4	2,516	227
D *By affiliation*										
Between independent companies	81.4	11.6	6.1	1.0	86.1	10.9	2.2	0.9	13,010	1,140
intra-MNC	54.9	39.3	5.8	–	79.5	16.1	4.5	–	3,394	112
E *By size of transaction:*										
Smallest 60%	86.2	11.4	2.1	0.3	88.2	9.7	1.7	0.4	959	751
Next 30%	84.4	12.4	1.8	1.4	83.2	13.3	1.9	1.6	3,170	376
Top 10%	72.9	19.0	7.4	0.6	76.0	15.2	8.0	0.8	12,276	123

Notes:
– = less than 0.05 (usually zero)
n.a. = not applicable
Detail may not add to 100 because of rounding
Source: Questionnaire survey

Table 4.2. *Currency of invoice, imports*

	Currency of invoice								Sample size	
	Percentage by value				Percentage by number of transactions					
			Third currency				Third currency			
	Seller's Currency	Pound	dollar	other	Seller's Currency	Pound	Dollar	Other	Value (£ thousands)	Number of transactions
A *Overall*	50.9	30.3	17.0	1.8	63.6	28.2	6.8	1.4	13,908	901
B *By trading partner:*										
Germany & Switzerland	68.1	29.9	1.2	0.8	89.0	9.8	0.6	0.6	1,168	163
Ireland & Channel Islands	–	–	–	–	–	–	–	–	0	0
Rest of EEC	52.5	33.8	12.5	1.2	71.7	25.1	2.3	0.9	2,778	219
Rest of W. Europe	52.1	41.9	5.5	0.5	54.5	36.8	6.4	2.4	1,293	125
E. Europe and USSR	–	51.6	11.6	36.8	–	80.0	6.7	13.3	503	30
Developed Sterling Area	24.4	72.4	3.2	–	25.0	69.4	5.6	–	384	36
USA	98.6	1.4	n.a.	–	94.4	5.6	n.a.	–	3,330	107
Canada	25.0	65.8	9.2	–	65.2	21.7	13.0	–	1,210	23
Latin America	1.5	12.4	86.0	–	5.9	35.3	58.8	–	1,627	17
Middle East	2.9	26.5	50.0	20.7	8.3	50.0	33.3	8.3	80	12
Africa, south of Sahara, exc. S. Africa	9.7	87.3	3.0	–	45.5	45.5	9.1	–	237	11
Japan and Hong Kong	47.9	33.6	18.6	–	63.8	28.8	7.5	–	697	80
Rest of world	14.3	56.2	29.1	0.4	25.6	47.4	24.4	2.6	599	78
C *By commodity:*										
SITC 0–1; Food, drink, tobacco	65.8	27.5	5.6	1.1	51.4	40.1	7.0	1.4	3,208	142
SITC 2 & 4; Raw materials	25.8	67.0	6.9	0.3	43.4	48.1	7.7	0.8	1,819	129
SITC 3; Fuels & lubricants	87.3	–	12.7	–	80.0	–	20.0	–	2,135	5
SITC 5; Chemicals	20.7	11.4	67.5	0.5	58.6	25.7	14.3	1.4	2,144	70
SITC 6; Manufactures classified by material	26.0	57.1	11.2	5.6	56.9	33.5	7.3	2.3	2,332	218

SITC 71–72; Machinery and electrical equip.	71.4	22.5	0.5	5.6	88.9	8.6	0.6	1.9	1,297	162
SITC 73; Vehicles exc. ships	42.5	51.3	6.2	–	66.7	28.6	4.8	–	215	21
SITC 8; Miscellaneous manufactures	74.6	17.4	7.8	0.2	76.0	15.6	7.8	0.6	758	154
Tradables I	40.6	28.7	27.3	3.5	70.6	21.3	6.5	1.7	6,216	601
Tradables II	59.3	31.5	8.7	0.5	49.7	42.0	7.3	1.0	7,692	300
D *By affiliation:*										
Between independent companies	48.3	29.0	19.8	2.9	64.5	26.9	7.1	1.5	8,391	744
Intra-MNC	54.8	32.2	12.7	0.2	59.2	34.4	5.1	1.3	5,516	157
E *By size of transaction:*										
Smallest 60%	67.6	26.3	5.5	0.6	71.2	23.7	4.1	1.1	994	541
Next 30%	56.4	31.4	10.6	1.6	55.2	33.3	10.0	1.5	2,692	270
Top 10%	47.8	30.4	19.8	2.0	43.3	40.0	13.3	3.3	10,222	90

Notes:
– = less than 0.05 (usually zero)
n.a. = not applicable
Detail may not add to 100 because of rounding
Source: Questionnaire survey

trade with different areas. In trade with the countries whose currencies are now thought of as having an important international role, i.e. the USA, Germany, and Switzerland, sterling invoicing of imports is markedly less prevalent than is buyer-currency invoicing of British exports. In these cases seller-currency invoicing of imports is overwhelming, and third-currency invoicing is of negligible importance for both exports and imports. With a second group of countries, comprising the rest of the EEC, Canada, and (a marginal case) Japan and Hong Kong, relationships appear truly symmetrical: the seller's currency accounts for some 75% of invoicing (give or take 10%), the buyer's currency for some 20% and third currency invoicing for the remaining 5% or so, on both sides of the account. In a third group of countries, represented by the rest of Western Europe (and possibly Japan and Hong Kong), seller-currency invoicing accounts for the bulk of imports and third-currency invoicing remains of modest importance, but there is no doubt that sterling plays a bigger role overall than does the partner's currency. In the fourth group of countries, represented by all other areas except Latin America, sterling invoicing is predominant for imports as well as exports – although in no case is it as dominant for imports as it is for exports – while third-currency invoicing remains small. In the final group of countries, represented by Latin America, the partner's currency is of negligible importance, but third-currency invoicing dominates with respect to imports.

The above findings suggest that the established practice of dichotomising currencies into those with and those without a vehicle-currency role may be too crude. At least insofar as invoicing practices are concerned, it would seem that currencies might more usefully and accurately be regarded as forming a hierarchy. The mid-1975 hierarchy suggested by our findings is as follows:

US dollar
Deutsche Mark and Swiss franc
Sterling and the currencies of other members of the EEC
Canadian dollar
Japanese yen
Currencies of other West European countries
Currencies of non-industrialized countries, including COMECON and the Developed Sterling Area.

The currencies at the top of the hierarchy are those with the most extensive international role, while those at the bottom are those which appear to have no international role at all. This 'hierarchical' view of the relative international roles of different currencies may be thought of as a third hypothesis, intermediate between the traditional 'vehicle currency hypothesis' and Grassman's 'symmetry hypothesis'.

Consider next the pattern of invoicing of exports by commodity

(Table 4.1, Section C). This pattern shows considerable volatility on the basis of value, but this is again largely due to the disproportionate impact of a handful of large transactions and so we concentrate attention on the data on the number of transactions. On that basis the striking feature shown by the commodity breakdown of exports is the uniformity of the proportion of sterling invoicing. With the exception of raw materials, where the buyer's currency has an unexpectedly large weight, and vehicles excluding ships, where the sterling proportion reaches 93%, all categories have between 80 and 90% of exports invoiced in sterling. The only commodity where there is any trace of the dollar playing a significant vehicle-currency role is fuel, and even there the sterling proportion is almost 85% (although the sample is very small). There is a rather general tendency, violated only in the cases of large capital goods and, very strikingly, fuel, for the percentage of the *number* of sterling-invoiced transactions to exceed the percentage of the *value* of sterling-invoiced transactions, i.e. for foreign currencies to play a greater role in invoicing large transactions. A similar phenomenon was found by Grassman for Sweden and is confirmed by Section E of the tables. The phenomenon is intuitively plausible: presumably small purchases are generally bought 'off the peg' on standard terms stipulated by the seller which include invoicing in his preferred (domestic) currency, while large purchases tend to be a matter for negotiation, which may include the currency of invoice.

The breakdown between exports of tradables I and II shows rather surprising results. Sterling does play a smaller – though not that much smaller – role in invoicing tradable II exports as measured by the number of transactions, but (a) this finding is reversed on the value measure, and (b) sterling is replaced by the buyer's currency rather than by the dollar playing a third-currency role.

There is somewhat more variability in the results for imports, but the overall picture is in most respects rather similar. If one excludes fuels and vehicles on the grounds that the sample sizes are too small, and again concentrates attention on the figures for the percentage of the number of transactions, one may observe the following similarities.

1. The proportion invoiced in the seller's currency is highest for finished manufactures (SITC 7–8), followed by manufactures that are predominantly intermediate goods (SITC 5–6), followed by food etc. (SITC 0–1), and finally by raw materials (SITC 2 and 4).
2. A reduction in the role of the seller's currency is matched principally by a rise in the use of the buyer's currency, sterling, rather than by greater use of third-currency invoicing – although chemicals provide something of an exception.
3. With the exceptions of food and the small-sample cases, the percent-

age invoiced in the seller's currency is higher on a number-of-transactions basis than on a value basis, suggesting again that large transactions are less likely to follow the simple routine of exporter-currency invoicing.

4. Tradables I are more prone to exporter-currency invoicing than are tradables II, but the latter are *not* more prone to third-currency invoicing.

The data on currency of invoicing by affiliation in Sections D show some tendency for the buyer's currency to play a greater role in intra-MNC transactions than in those between independent firms. Perhaps surprisingly, given that the dollar is presumably the home currency of many of the multinationals, there is no systematic tendency for the US dollar to play a more important third-currency role in intra-MNC transactions.

The data on currency of invoicing by size of transactions shown in Sections E display a quite strong tendency for the exporter's currency to be used to a greater extent in the smaller transactions. Conversely, third currencies, and particularly the US dollar, play a markedly larger role in the invoicing of the larger transactions. As already noted, this is neither unexpected nor implausible.

Data on the use of the US dollar in invoicing British foreign trade are brought together in Table 4.3. The overall impression conveyed by these figures is similar to the conclusion reached by Grassman on the basis of his Swedish data: that, although the dollar plays a significant role on the import side, it is very far from being a dominant vehicle currency.

Table 4.4 presents the results of our survey regarding the use of the forward market for covering exports. About 15% of the value of exports invoiced in foreign currencies were covered forward (amounting to less

Table 4.3. *Use of the US dollar in invoicing UK foreign trade*

(*Percentages*)

	Exports		Imports	
	Value	No. of transactions	Value	No. of transactions
As seller's currency	n.a.	n.a.	23.6	11.2
As buyer's currency	1.3	1.8	n.a.	n.a.
As third currency	6.0	2.4	17.0	6.8
Total	7.3	4.2	40.6	18.0
Tradables I	7.0	3.2	37.5	19.6
Tradables II	9.2	8.8	43.2	14.7
Between independent firms	7.7	4.2	40.4	16.3
Intra-MNC	5.8	4.5	41.0	26.1

Source: Questionnaire survey

Table 4.4. *Forward covering of UK exports*

	Percentage of total exports		Percentage of FX-invoiced exports		Sample size[a]	
	Value	No. of transactions	Value	No. of transactions	Value (£ thousands)	No. of transactions
Overall	3.7	1.9	15.5	13.2	3,951	182
Tradables I	3.5	0.9	14.6	7.7	3,379	124
Tradables II	4.7	6.6	20.8	25.9	572	58
Between ind. firms	4.6	1.9	24.6	13.8	2,421	159
Intra-MNC	0.4	1.8	1.0	8.7	1,529	23
Trads. I/ind. firms	4.6	1.0	26.1	8.6	1,884	105
Trads. I/MNC	–	–	–	–	1,495	19
Trads. II/ind. firms	4.6	6.2	19.3	24.1	538	54
Trads. II/MNC	6.4	11.1	43.1	50.0	34	4
By size of transaction:						
smallest 60%	1.8	1.3	13.0	11.2	132	89
next 30%	2.8	2.9	17.9	17.5	495	63
largest 10%	4.1	2.4	15.2	10.0	3,324	30

Notes:
[a]These two columns refer to the value and number of foreign-currency-invoiced exports, i.e. they provide the sample size for the preceding two columns rather than for the first two (which can be found from Table 4.1).
Source: Questionnaire survey

than 4% of total exports), which is low compared to other figures that have been found (see Table 2.4, p. 25) especially considering that the pound was floating (none too smoothly) at the time of the survey. The proportion of tradable II exports covered was higher than of tradables I, and independent firms were more prone to cover than were MNCs in internal transactions. Two cases of intra-MNC covering did, however, occur, and since both were in tradable II exports they led to a spectacular 50% rate of cover in intra-MNC foreign exchange-invoiced tradable II export transactions (of which there were only four altogether). Obviously the small size of the sample means that this result cannot be taken seriously. Although the proportion of total exports covered forward rose with the size of the transaction, the proportion of foreign-currency-invoiced exports scarcely did; the fact that transactions covered forward tend to be drawn from the larger transactions was apparently merely a reflection of the fact that it is the larger transactions that are more likely to be invoiced in foreign currency, rather than that a greater absolute exposure to foreign exchange risk provided a greater incentive to go to the additional trouble of using the forward market.

The overall rate of forward covering was somewhat higher on the import than on the export side (see Table 4.5), involving 22% of the transactions exposed to exchange risk and 36% of the value of those

Table 4.5. *Forward covering of UK imports*

	Percentage of total imports		Percentage of FX-invoiced imports		Sample size[a]	
	Value	No. of transactions	Value	No. of transactions	Value (£ thousands)	No. of transactions
Overall	25.3	15.4	36.3	21.5	9,698	647
Tradables I	25.6	14.1	35.9	18.0	4,430	473
Tradables II	25.1	18.0	36.6	31.0	5,268	174
Between ind. firms	38.2	16.3	53.8	22.2	5,960	544
Intra-MNC	5.7	11.5	8.4	19.4	3,737	103
Trads. I/ind. firms	37.9	14.7	45.6	18.3	3,233	387
Trads. I/intra-MNC	5.0	11.9	9.7	16.3	1,197	86
Trads. II/Ind. firms	38.5	19.2	63.4	31.8	2,728	157
Trads. II/intra-MNC	6.1	10.3	7.7	23.5	2,541	17
By size of transaction:						
smallest 60%	15.9	13.3	21.5	17.4	732	413
next 30%	18.9	18.5	27.5	27.8	1,846	180
largest 10%	27.9	18.9	40.1	31.5	7,119	54

Note:
[a]These two columns refer to the value and number of foreign-currency-invoiced imports, i.e. they provide the sample size for the previous two columns rather than for the first two.
Source: Questionnaire survey

transactions. Contrary to what we had expected on the basis of the theory outlined in Chapter 1, tradable I imports were *not* more prone to be covered forward than were those of tradables II; indeed, the contrary was true on the basis of the number (as opposed to value) of transactions. The value figures suggest strong support for the hypothesis that intra-MNC trade is less likely to be covered forward than is that between independent firms; but the figures for the number of transactions, which we have argued are in general more reliable and deserve to be taken more seriously, do not. We return to consider these paradoxical results at greater length in the second part of this chapter.

The final part of Table 4.5 shows that on the import side at least there is a fairly pronounced tendency for a larger proportion of the bigger transactions to be covered forward. This suggests that the 'value' figures are probably more useful than the 'number of transactions' figures in providing overall estimates of the proportion of imports that is covered forward.

As noted in Section 2.2, forward covering is not the only possible method of gaining protection against risk. In fact our questionnaire contained two questions (C.3 and C.5) designed to yield information on the prevalence of other techniques. In response to the question as to whether foreign exchange risk had been reduced by any technique other than forward covering, such as borrowing or matching, we obtained the responses shown in the third row of Table 4.6, which draws together our

Table 4.6. *Methods of reducing foreign exchange risk*

(*Percentages*)

	Exports		Imports	
	By value	By no. of transactions	By value	By no. of transactions
Sterling invoicing	75.9	85.5	30.3	28.2
Covered forward	3.7	1.9	25.3	15.4
'Other method'	7.9	1.7	5.2	3.8
Residual: exposed to exchange risk	12.5	10.9	39.2	52.6

Source: Questionnaire survey

results concerning the various possible methods of reducing exchange risk. It turned out that for exports these 'other methods' were collectively of the same order of importance as forward covering, which made us wish that we had asked our respondents to specify what 'other method' they had in fact used.

The last line of Table 4.6 is also interesting. Despite the fairly limited use made of the forward market, it is reasonably clear that the bulk of UK trade by value does not involve the British trader in holding a position exposed to foreign exchange risk. Perhaps 75% of British trade overall is free of exchange risk to the British trader. By far the most important way of avoiding risk is sterling invoicing. Of course, if all trade were invoiced in either the seller's or the buyer's currency, then 50% of world trade overall would necessarily be 'free of exchange risk' in this sense – i.e. each transaction would involve risk to only one party.

The question asking whether the contract contained any clauses

Table 4.7. *Clauses to guard against changes in production or trading conditions*

(*Percentages*)

	Exports		Imports	
	By value	By no. of transactions	By value	By no. of transactions
None	72.7	85.5	98.3	96.1
Cost escalation clause only	26.1	12.9	0.6	1.1
Exchange clause only	0.1	0.5	0.6	1.5
Both cost escalation and exchange clauses	0.1	0.2	0.2	0.6
Unspecified clauses	1.0	0.9	0.3	0.7

Source: Questionnaire survey

guarding against changes in production or trading conditions elicited the responses shown in Table 4.7. A number of the 'cost-escalation clauses', particularly for low-value transactions where a customer was buying goods off the shelf at a list price, merely stipulated that the price was that ruling at the date of despatch. Even allowing for this qualification, however, cost-escalation clauses appear to cover a significant proportion of UK exports, although not of imports. Exchange clauses were, as we had expected, very uncommon.

4.2 Hypothesis testing

In the preceding section we presented our results with only the occasional reference to their apparent consistency or otherwise with the series of hypotheses about the determinants of the currency of invoice and use of the forward market that were developed in Section 1.2. In the present section we turn to systematic testing of those hypotheses on the basis of the data generated by our questionnaire.

Hypothesis I 'Tradables I exported to an independent firm from a country with a convertible currency will be invoiced in the exporter's currency.'

It has already been noted that data such as those shown in Table 2.1 (pp. 18–19) show a widespread pattern among industrial countries, all of which have convertible currencies, for their own currency to be the most important single currency in which exports are invoiced, usually – and especially for the larger countries – by a wide margin. It was indeed the discovery of this empirical regularity by Grassman that prompted McKinnon's theoretical work which was summarised by Section 1.2 and from which the present hypothesis is drawn. Our own overall results reported in Tables 4.1, Section A and 4.2, Section A are consistent with this pattern. Even before sorting out tradables II and intra-MNC transactions, or devising any rigorous tests, we therefore start off with a strong presumption that this hypothesis will receive support.

We have already described (Section 3.5) our basis for classifying goods as between the two categories tradables I and II. It will be recalled that the former are basically manufactured goods (SITC 5–8 excluding 67–68) while the latter are primary products (SITC 0–4) and the semi-processed metals (SITC 67–68). So far as affiliation is concerned, our questionnaire contained a question (Question A.4) that revealed whether the transaction was between independent firms or between two branches of a MNC. The only remaining problem in sorting out these transactions to which Hypothesis I applies from those to which it does not is therefore that of deciding whether the exporter was located in a country with a convertible currency. This is trivial on the export side, since sterling is

than the observation that most behaviour is consistent with it. Consider the following approach. Suppose that all trade was necessarily invoiced in the currency of one or other of the trading partners. If there were no economic rationale to invoicing patterns, and the choice of invoice currency was entirely random, one would expect to observe about 50% of all transactions invoiced in the exporter's currency. One could therefore test Hypothesis I by examining whether the proportion of transactions invoiced in the exporter's currency was, on the usual statistical criteria, significantly greater than 50%. Now in fact there are well over 100 other currencies, apart from those of the seller and the buyer, that could in principle be used as the invoice currency (not to mention currency composites). Their existence must depress the proportion of invoicing in the exporter's currency that would arise through chance. Hence, if one finds that significantly more than 50% of the relevant transactions were invoiced in the exporter's currency one may be even more confident that this reflects the economic forces that suggest Hypothesis I than one would be in a 2-currency world; the 50% criterion provides an over-strong test of the hypothesis. This is therefore the first test that we adopt. The method by which we apply it is to look at the numbers of transactions invoiced in the exporter's currency and in other currencies respectively (shown in the last two columns of Table 4.8) in the cases where Hypothesis I is expected to apply (rows 1, 3 and 5), and ask whether these figures could have been generated by a binomial distribution with probabilities of 0.5 for both categories of invoicing. Given the sample sizes, the binomial distribution can of course be approximated by the normal. We call this Test A. Except where otherwise noted, we conduct our tests at the 1% significance level.

By Test A, 'other UK exports' (Table 4.8, row 2) would also be accepted as predominantly invoiced in the exporter's currency, despite the fact that for one reason or another they do not satisfy the conditions necessary for Hypothesis I to apply. Of course there is nothing in the theory which says that such exports should *not* be invoiced in sterling. For example, the pound is still to some extent a vehicle currency, so there is nothing inconsistent in tradable II exports being invoiced in sterling, and the theory does not predict that MNCs will *avoid* the use of the currency of the exporter for invoicing tradables I. Nevertheless, the theory would be somewhat unconvincing if exporter-currency invoicing were as common when the conditions that lead one to expect it to be dominant are absent as when they are present. In fact it is not as common; comparison between rows 1 and 2, 3, and 4, and 5 and 6 of Table 4.8 shows that exporter-currency invoicing is consistently more common when the conditions for Hypothesis I to apply are present than when they are not. Our second test is designed to establish whether those differences are statistically significant. For this purpose we apply the *chi-*

Table 4.9. *Tests of Hypothesis I*

	Test A		Test B	
	Actual	Critical value	Actual	Critical value
UK exports	826	504.9	31.03	6.63
UK imports	336	234.8	96.67	6.63
Total UK trade	1,162	721.3	195.1	6.63

Source: Table 4.8.

square test for homogeneity to the data shown in the final two columns of Table 4.8 for the three pairs of rows. We call this Test B.

The six results of applying these two tests in each of three cases (for exports, imports, and the two combined to give total trade) are shown in Table 4.9. Test A for exports is whether significantly more than 50% of the 931 export transactions to which Hypothesis I applies are invoiced in sterling. At the 1% level that test would be satisfied if more than 504.9 were invoiced in sterling; in fact no less than 826 were, so that the test is decisively positive. Test B for exports is whether a significantly higher proportion of exports is invoiced in sterling when the conditions specified by Hypothesis I are present than when they are absent, and is satisfied at the 1% level (given that there is only one degree of freedom) if *chi*-square exceeds 6.63. In fact it is 31.03 so this test is also decisively positive. The other four tests likewise proved emphatically positive. Hypothesis I could hardly be more strongly supported.

Hypothesis II 'Tradables II will be invoiced in a vehicle currency (dollars or sterling).'

Table 4.10 displays the proportions of trade in our samples that were invoiced in dollars and sterling, classified as between tradables I and II. We sum the proportions invoiced in dollars and sterling in order to get

Table 4.10. *UK trade invoiced in vehicle and other currencies*

		Percentage by value			Percentage by number of transactions		
		Dollar	Pound	Vehicle currencies	Dollar	Pound	Vehicle currencies
Exports:	Trads. I	7.0	75.7	82.7	3.2	87.9	91.1
	Trads. II	9.2	77.3	86.5	8.8	74.5	83.3
Imports:	Trads. I	37.5	28.7	66.2	19.6	21.3	40.9
	Trads. II	43.2	31.5	74.7	14.7	42.0	56.7
Total:	Trads. I	16.4	61.2	77.6	9.3	63.3	72.6
	Trads. II	34.8	42.8	77.6	12.1	56.0	68.1

Source: Questionnaire survey

the proportion invoiced in vehicle currencies. This might seem somewhat dubious in view of our finding reported earlier in this chapter that the pound's international role is now less than that of certain other European currencies, notably the Deutsche Mark and Swiss franc. However, the international commodity markets continue to operate in either the dollar or the pound, or both, and so it seems appropriate to continue treating the pound as one of the two vehicle currencies for the purpose of tradables II.

It will be observed that in every case the majority of tradables II (by both value and number of transactions) were invoiced in a vehicle currency. This proportion is not, however, uniformly higher than the proportion for tradables I. On the contrary, for the total sample the proportions are identical by value and actually lower for tradables II by number of transactions. In the case of the result by value, the proportion invoiced in a vehicle currency is higher for tradables II for both exports and imports, and the overall equality is a result of differential weighting. (75% of tradables II were imports, as against only 31% of tradables I.) By number of transactions, however, a *higher* proportion of tradables I than of tradables II were invoiced in a vehicle currency. This was, however, more than accounted for by the greater role of the *pound* in invoicing tradables I, as predicted by Hypothesis I. It follows that Hypothesis II cannot be tested by comparing the proportions of British *exports* of tradables I and II that are invoiced in vehicle as opposed to other currencies: in this case Hypotheses I and II give contradictory predictions, and a test may merely provide a measure of which of the two hypotheses is better supported than of whether they are both true. For the same reason, tests based on total trade make no sense. We therefore restrict our tests of this hypothesis to the results on imports.

If all tradable II imports were invoiced randomly in the currency of one or other trading partner, one would expect all imports from the USA and 50% of all other imports to be invoiced in a vehicle currency (given that the two currencies being treated as vehicle currencies are the dollar and the pound). Imports from the US are therefore in a special category, and are for that

Table 4.11. *UK imports from countries other than the USA by currency of invoice*

	Number of transactions invoiced in			
	Dollar	Pound	Total vehicle currencies	Other currencies
Tradables I	39	124	163	355
Tradables II	22	124	146	130

Source: Questionnaire survey

reason excluded from the data that will be used to test Hypothesis II (Table 4.11). One might proceed to use these data in order to apply Test A as before, to examine whether significantly more than 50% of tradable II imports (from countries other than the USA) were invoiced in a vehicle currency. However, the bias in that criterion arising from the existence of more than two currencies may make this an over-weak test in the present context rather than an over-strong one as before, in as much as (to the extent that the additional invoice currency is in fact the other vehicle currency) more than 50% of contracts would be invoiced in a vehicle currency even though the choice of invoice currency were random. An over-strong test could be constructed by assuming that the population of invoice currencies were three (dollar, sterling, and exporter's), and testing whether the observed distribution between vehicle and other currencies could have been generated by chance if the probability of selecting each of the eligible currencies were equal. Satisfaction of this test would require that the proportion of vehicle-currency invoices be significantly greater than two thirds; since it is in fact only 53%, this over-strong test fails. (It may be noted, however, that some 61% of the relevant imports by value were invoiced in a vehicle currency.)

We are therefore restricted to applying a Type B test. We use a *chi*-square test to see whether the higher proportion of vehicle-currency invoicing for tradables II as opposed to tradables I shown in Table 4.11 could have arisen by chance had the two samples been drawn from a common population. The value of *chi*-square is in fact 45.9, as against a critical value of 9.2 at the one per cent significance level. The greater propensity to invoice tradable II imports in a vehicle currency is therefore confirmed as statistically significant. However, it has to be admitted that this is entirely because of heavier use of the pound, rather than of the dollar (whose proportionate use is in fact almost exactly what would be expected if there were no differences in invoicing practices between tradables I and II, as reflected in a negligible contribution of the dollar to the value of *chi*-square). One must therefore conclude that, while Hypothesis II receives some support from the data, this support is rather weak.

It is possible that our failure to find strong confirmation for Hypothesis II is not because the underlying theory is incorrect, but because our classification of goods between tradables I and II on the basis of 1-digit SITC classes was too crude. We had of course expected that SITC 0–1, in particular, would include a number of tradable I commodities (whisky, chocolates, etc.), and there is some suggestion in Table 4.2, Section C that a number of other intermediate goods beside SITC 67–68, notably chemicals, may share the invoicing patterns that we argued could be expected to characterise homogeneous primary commodities. A natural check therefore seemed to be to extract these ambiguous cases and consider just the results for those SITC numbers that it would seem

Table 4.12. *Restricted sample of UK imports from countries other than the USA by currency of invoice*

	Number of transactions invoiced in			
	Dollar	Pound	Total vehicle currencies	Other currencies
SITC 7 & 8 (trads. I)	14	42	56	214
SITC 2 & 4 (trads. II)	10	61	71	47

Source: Questionnaire survey

possible to assign unambiguously between tradables I and II. Table 4.12 therefore shows data similar to those displayed in Table 4.11, but confined to SITC 7 and 8 (tradables I) and SITC 2 and 4 (tradables II).

It is apparent from Table 4.12 that vehicle-currency invoicing is indeed more prevalent in the invoicing of imports of SITC 2 & 4 than of imports of SITC 7 & 8. The proportion of transactions invoiced in a vehicle currency is 60% in the first case as against only 21% in the second; while sterling invoicing accounts for the bulk of this difference, dollar invoicing is also somewhat higher for SITC 2 & 4. (Proportions by value are 75% for tradables II as against 31% vehicle-currency invoicing for unambiguous tradables I.) The difference between the two rows is highly significant; the value of *chi*-square is 60.8, while the critical value at the one per cent significance level is 9.2. We therefore conclude that Hypothesis II appears to be consistent with the evidence, especially when it is interpreted more narrowly to apply only to raw materials rather than to our original basis of classification tradables I and II.

Hypothesis IIA 'The vehicle currency used for invoicing commodities traded on an international market will be the currency of the country where the market for the commodity in question is located.'

The number of transactions that involved commodities that we were

Table 4.13. *Invoiced currencies for commodities traded on an international market*

Invoice currency	Market in USA	Market in UK	Markets in USA & UK
Dollar	5	1	1
Pound	5	3	6
Other	1	1	2

Source: Questionnaire survey

able to identify as traded on an international market proved remarkably small (Table 4.13). Furthermore, nine of the 25 transactions that were so identified involved commodities for which active international markets exist in both Britain and the United States. There are therefore only 16 cases in which our hypothesis yields a prediction as to whether the dollar or the pound is more likely to be used as the invoice currency.

It can be seen from Table 4.13 that there is some tendency for commodities to be invoiced more heavily in the currency of the country where the international market in question is located, as predicted, but that this is by no means an invariable practice. Given the small size of the sample, the tendency to invoice more heavily in the predicted direction is statistically quite insignificant.

Hypothesis III 'Tradables I exported to another branch of the same MNC are less likely to be invoiced in the home currency of the exporter than are tradables I exports sold to an independent firm.'

It is straightforward to test this hypothesis. It specifically refers to the difference in tradable I invoicing practices to be expected in intra-MNC as opposed to other transactions, and Test B is therefore called for. The relevant data are exhibited in Table 4.14 and exhibit the predicted tendency for independent firms to use the exporter's currency more often. The *chi*-square test just failed to be significant (at the one per cent level) on the export side (Table 4.15). The tendency in the predicted direction is much less pronounced, and clearly statistically insignificant, on the import side. However, combining the two samples gives a value of *chi*-square of 13.7, as against the critical value of 6.6. Furthermore, the data

Table 4.14. *Percentage of tradables I invoiced in exporter's currency, classified by affiliation*

	Percentage by value	Percentage by number of transactions	Number of transactions	Number of other transactions[a]
Exports:				
intra-MNC	52.7	79.8	75	19
ind. firms	82.4	88.7	826	105
Imports:				
intra-MNC	35.4	66.1	78	40
ind. firms	43.6	71.6	346	137
Total trade:				
intra-MNC	45.4	72.2	153	59
ind. firms	72.1	82.9	1,172	242

Source: Questionnaire survey
Note:
[a] Number of transactions in tradables I not invoiced in exporter's currency

Table 4.15. *Tests of Hypothesis III (Test B)*

	Actual *chi*-square	Critical value
Exports	6.41	6.63
Imports	1.40	6.63
Total trade	13.70	6.63

Source: Table 4.14

on trade values show a markedly larger dispersion between the practices of intra-MNC and other invoicing than do those on the number of transactions on which the significance tests are based. We therefore regard this hypothesis as strongly supported by the data.

Hypothesis IV 'Tradables I imported from countries with inconvertible currencies will be invoiced in either sterling or dollars, with the sterling-invoiced proportion higher than in imports from countries with convertible currencies.'

The data on the proportion of British imports of tradables I that were invoiced in sterling, dollars and other currencies, classified by the convertibility or otherwise of the currency of the exporter, are shown in Table 4.16. It can be seen that only 12% of imports from countries with inconvertible currencies by value, and 23% by number of transactions, were not invoiced in either the pound or the dollar. These figures are far below those of 43% and 64% found in imports from countries with convertible currencies. We again applied Test B to see whether the difference in terms of the number of transactions was statistically significant according to the *chi*-square test. The value of *chi*-square was in fact 70.5, as compared to the critical value of 9.2 at the one per cent level (with two degrees of freedom). Furthermore virtually all of this was accounted for by the sterling and other-invoiced proportions: the dollar column accounted for only 4.4 of the total of 70.5. This implies that the dollar proportion was essentially the same as between imports from countries with and without convertible currencies, and hence that it is

Table 4.16. *Invoicing of tradable I imports by currency-type of exporter*

	Percentage by value			Percentage by number of transactions			No. of transactions		
Currency-type of exporter	Pound	Dollar	Other	Pound	Dollar	Other	Pound	Dollar	Other
Inconvertible	5.9	81.8	12.3	45.1	32.4	22.5	32	23	16
Convertible	38.3	18.7	42.9	18.1	17.9	64.0	96	95	339

Source: Questionnaire survey

the sterling-invoiced proportion that is higher in imports from countries with inconvertible currencies. The hypothesis therefore appears consistent with the data. (The one reservation that should be noted is that the data on *value* show a very different picture to those on the number of transactions, with the role of the pound dropping even more than that of 'other currencies', and the dollar assuming an overwhelming role for invoicing imports from inconvertible-currency countries. This result would contradict the second part of the hypothesis, but be perfectly consistent with the first part. However, we do not attach great importance to the results by value, for reasons explained previously.)

Hypothesis V 'Importers of tradables I invoiced in a foreign currency are more likely to cover forward than are importers of tradables II invoiced in a foreign currency.'

Data relevant to testing this hypothesis are displayed in Table 4.17. The first section of the table shows the percentages of foreign-currency-invoiced trade covered forward, by value and by number of transactions, for all trade, classified as between tradables I and II. It will be observed that the proportions by value are virtually identical, while by number of transactions the proportion of tradables II covered is distinctly *higher*, rather than lower as predicted by the hypothesis. However, it can be argued that, since Hypothesis VI predicts that intra-MNC transactions will not be covered forward even for tradables I, it would be appropriate to omit all intra-MNC transactions for the purpose of testing this

Table 4.17. *Foreign-currency-invoiced imports covered forward*

	Percentage by value	Percentage by number of transactions	Number of transactions	Number of other transactions[a]
All transactions:				
tradables I	35.9	18.0	85	388
tradables II	36.6	31.0	54	120
Non-affiliates only:				
tradables I	45.6	18.3	71	317
tradables II	63.4	31.8	50	107
All transactions:				
SITC 7 & 8	17.5	16.0	47	246
SITC 2 & 4	41.8	38.8	26	41
Non-affiliates only:				
SITC 7 & 8	18.4	15.5	36	197
SITC 2 & 4	42.5	39.7	25	38

Note:
[a] Number of foreign-currency-invoiced import transactions not covered forward
Source: Questionnaire survey

hypothesis. Accordingly, this is done in the second section of the table. It is clear that the new data are even less consistent with the hypothesis than the original set; the proportion by number of transactions is virtually unchanged, while that by value is now also opposite to that predicted by the hypothesis. We found reason to believe earlier, however, that our distinction between tradables I and II did not perfectly correspond to the theoretical distinction, and we performed certain calculations using the more restricted samples of SITC 7 & 8 and 2 & 4 instead. The bottom half of Table 4.17 therefore presents the same information as the top half, but on the basis of this more restricted coverage.

It can be seen that the data on the more restricted basis are even more strongly contrary to the hypothesis, and eliminating intra-MNC transactions slightly reinforces rather than weakens this finding. Furthermore, the tendency for tradables II to be more heavily covered forward is statistically highly significant: the value of *chi*-square varies between 11.9 and 17.8, as against the critical value of 6.6 at the one per cent level with one degree of freedom. We are therefore driven to the conclusion that our original hypothesis was incorrect and that there is a significant tendency for traders to cover tradables II more frequently than tradables I. We do not have an explanation of this empirical finding readily at hand.

Hypothesis VI 'Except when the central bank is supporting the forward rate, intra-MNC transactions are less likely to be covered forward than are transactions between independent firms.'

There was no Bank of England support for the forward rate during the relatively tranquil period on which our investigation focussed, so we can test this hypothesis by comparing the extent of forward cover on foreign

Table 4.18. *Forward cover on foreign-currency-invoiced trade classified by affiliation*

	Percentage by value	Percentage by number of transactions	No. of transactions	No. of other transactions[a]
Exports: intra-MNC	1.0	8.7	2	21
ind. firms	24.6	13.8	22	137
Imports: intra-MNC	8.4	17.5	18	85
ind. firms	53.8	22.2	121	423
Total trade: intra-MNC	6.2	15.9	20	106
ind. firms	45.4	20.3	143	560

Note:

[a] Number of foreign-currency-invoiced transactions not covered forward
Source: Questionnaire survey

Table 4.19. *Tests of Hypothesis VI (Test B)*

	Actual *chi*-square	Critical value
Exports[a]	0.12	6.63
Imports	1.15	6.63
Total trade	1.34	6.63

Note:
[a] Yates' correction for continuity was applied in this test in view of the small sample size. The purpose of the correction is to compensate for the fact that the frequencies used are discrete in nature, whereas the *chi*-square distribution is continuous. The correction reduces the absolute difference between the observed frequency (f_0) and the expected frequency (f_e) by one half; symbolically,

$$\chi^2 = \frac{\Sigma(|f_0 - f_e| - 0.5)^2}{f_e}$$

When expected frequencies are large, the correction would have a negligible effect, and it may therefore be dispensed with. But in the present test, with the small expected frequency for exports ($f_e = 3$), the difference is important. See Kazmier (1973).
Source: Table 4.18.

currency-invoiced transactions on intra-MNC as opposed to other trade. The relevant data are presented in Table 4.18. It may be remarked that we had initially planned to confine attention on the import side to tradables I, since we had argued that for tradables II price risk would offset exchange risk for all importers and that there should therefore be no difference between the behaviour in intra-MNC and other transactions, but in view of our earlier failure to find a lesser tendency for the importers of tradables II to cover forward, this seemed inappropriate.

It will be observed that the proportion of intra-MNC trade covered forward is consistently lower than the proportion of trade between independent firms that is covered. The difference is quite dramatic when the comparison is made in terms of value of trade, but marginal in terms of the percentage of transactions. (The difference remains in the predicted direction, but is even more marginal in magnitude, when the comparisons are made in terms of tradables I alone rather than in terms of all imports.) As Table 4.19 shows, none of the differences, in terms of the number of transactions, is statistically significant. Given our test procedures, we clearly cannot claim to have assembled any support for the hypothesis. Nevertheless, in view of the results by value, we are not persuaded that it should be rejected.

4.3 Conclusions

In Chapter 1 we developed six hypotheses as to the determinants of currency of invoice and use of the forward market. The data collected in our sample provided strong statistical support for four of these – Hypotheses I, II, III and IV. A further two hypotheses, IIA and VI, were consistent with the data but did not receive statistical confirmation. Hypothesis V was rejected.

It may be useful to provide a summary of what we have been able to establish in the way of knowledge of the topics covered in this chapter. This knowledge derives both from the hypotheses subjected to formal tests, and from the examination of the statistical results presented previously.

First, there is overwhelming evidence that the normal practice in exporting manufactured products is to invoice in the exporter's currency (Hypothesis I), except when that currency is inconvertible (Hypothesis IV). However, normal practice is not invariably followed. Practice is more likely to deviate from this norm (a) the higher is the importer's currency relative to the exporter's currency in the 'hierarchy of currencies' (p. 62); (b) for transactions between the branches of a MNC (Hypothesis III); (c) the larger the value of the transaction (Tables 4.1, Section E and 4.2, Section E); and perhaps (d) for intermediate products (Table 4.2, Section C). When the exporter's currency is not used, the buyer's currency is the usual alternative. When a third currency is used, which is usually in trade with inconvertible-currency countries, it is most likely to be the US dollar. However, even a currency like the Malawi kwacha may be used as a third currency on occasion.

Second, practices differ in the invoicing of raw materials – even though not perhaps as much as we had originally been expecting. Our tests of Hypothesis II provided confirmation that trade in raw materials is more likely to make use of a vehicle currency, and there does seem to be some tendency (although it was not statistically confirmed in the test of Hypothesis IIA) to use the currency of the country where the commodity market is located in the invoicing of commodities traded on an international market. There remains an open question as to just where the boundaries between tradables I and II ought to be drawn in statistical terms.

Third, we found that the British trader is exposed to exchange risk on something over 10% of exports and perhaps 40% of imports (Table 4.6). By far the most important method of avoiding exchange risk, even for imports, is sterling invoicing, followed by forward covering. We have not, however, had great success in explaining why firms sometimes choose to cover and sometimes do not. The evidence is consistent with, but does not provide statistical support for, the hypothesis that intra-MNC transactions are less likely to be covered (Hypothesis IV). It is inconsistent with the hypothesis that tradables II are less likely to be covered than tradables I (Hypothesis V), which would seem to be rational behaviour in a world where exchange-rate fluctuations cause parallel fluctuations in the sterling price of imports of tradables II. We do not know whether to blame the rejection of this hypothesis on a quirk of our sample, irrationality on the part of British traders, or an inadequacy of the economic reasoning that led us to Hypothesis V; but the topic is discussed further in Chapter 7.

No doubt both the topics covered in this chapter would benefit from further research. However, the need would seem to be vastly more acute in the case of forward cover than in regard to choice of invoice currency. In the latter case, theory led to a series of non-trivial theorems which were found to be decisively supported by the data of our sample.

5

METHODS OF SETTLEMENT AND CREDIT TERMS

This chapter comprises the reporting, discussion and analysis of our findings on the methods of settlement and credit terms that are used in British foreign trade. It falls naturally into two sections. In the first we set out our findings on the use of methods of settlement, note points of interest, and test hypotheses against the data. The second part comprises a report and discussion of our findings on credit terms.

5.1 Methods of settlement[1]

Our overall findings on the frequency of the various methods of settlement distinguished in Section 3.1 are displayed in Table 5.1, together with Grassman's comparable findings for Swedish trade in 1968. It can be seen that, as Grassman found in Sweden, open account is the single most important method of settlement. However, it is quite clear that open account does not have anything like the same dominance in the settlement of British trade as it does in Sweden: the proportion of exports settled on open account is scarcely more than half as large in the UK as it is in Sweden. The smaller use of open account in Britain is reflected principally in greater use of acceptance bills, sight documentary credits, and instalments (on the export side), and of cash against documents (on the import side).[2]

By comparing the percentage of export (or import) contracts using a particular method of settlement with the percentage of the value of exports (or imports) using the method, one can draw inferences about whether particular methods of settlement tend to be used more frequently for large or small transactions. Table 5.1 suggests several tendencies. Most conspicuously, the export data suggest that open account tends to be used for small transactions and instalments for large transactions. Both of these findings are plausible: one would expect the simple but relatively less secure procedures of open account to be used most readily where the sums at stake are modest, and one would expect instalments to be used for payments for large and expensive capital goods. What is perhaps surprising is that there is so little evidence of

Table 5.1. *Methods of settlement in British foreign trade*

Row no.	Methods of settlement (1)	Percentage of: Export contracts (2)	Value of exports (3)	Value of Swedish exports (4)	Import contracts (5)	Value of imports (6)	Value of Swedish imports (7)
1	Open account	39.5	23.9		38.2	39.1	68.5
2	Periodic settlement	5.9	3.2	52.9	6.4	3.5	
3	Cash on delivery	2.5	4.1		6.5	4.6	
4	Cash against documents	13.8	16.6	21.2	17.6	32.2	10.5
5	Payment of bills against documents	4.3	2.1		2.0	1.5	
6	Sight documentary credits	10.5	15.2	3.4	6.3	3.5	1.6
7	Acceptance of bills against documents	16.5	9.9	4.9	13.4	7.4	6.3
8	Time documentary credits	2.6	1.7	1.2	6.8	4.5	1.6
9	Advance (full amount)	1.2	0.1	0.6	0.4	negligible	2.3
10	Advance (prior to instalments)	1.8	8.0	11.8	0.8	0.4	6.0
11	Instalments	1.3	13.3		0.6	2.5	
12	Consignment	0.2	1.8	2.1	0.9	0.8	1.7
13	Free deliveries			2.1			1.5
	Memorandum items						
	No credit (rows 3, 4, 5, 6, 9)	32.3	38.1	25.2	32.8	41.8	14.4
	Fixed credit (rows 7, 8, 10, 11)	22.2	32.9	17.9	21.6	14.8	13.9
	Variable credit (rows 1, 2, 12)	45.6	28.9	55.0	45.5	43.4	70.2
	Sample size	1252	£16,404,423	Kr. 24,580m.	901	£13,907,639	Kr. 26,163m.

Sources: Columns 2, 3, 5, 6, – Questionnaire survey; Columns 4, 7 – Grassman (1973a, Table 2.4, p. 28)

similar effects, particularly regarding the use of open account, on the import side. It may also be noted that periodic settlement and acceptance bills seems to be more heavily used in the smaller contracts, while, especially on the import side, cash against documents is more used in the larger contracts.

In Chapter 1.2 we developed two hypotheses about the use of the various available methods of settlement. We now proceed to test these two hypotheses against the data. The first step is to rank the twelve methods of settlement distinguished in Table 5.1 by the flexibility they offer the buyer in choosing when to settle the account.

As has already been indicated, there is no doubt that the most flexible method is open account. In its pure form this involves the seller sending an invoice which simply specifies that payment must be made by a certain date. The variation on this method, which comprises an agreement that payments be made by the buyer on a regular periodic basis, does not in principle allow the same flexibility to choose the date of payment. However, it seems that in practice this provision is usually applied informally and changes in the timing of payments are usually possible within limits if the buyer decides that this is in his interest. We therefore add periodic settlement to open account as a 'flexible' method of settlement.

The other methods of settlement offer much less flexibility. They differ among themselves more in the length of the *period of credit* they provide than in how free they leave the buyer to choose when he will make payment. These other methods are cash on delivery, cash against documents,[3] payment of bills against documents, sight documentary credits, acceptance of bills against documents, time documentary credits, and instalments. Payment in advance is also included here in our tests because it does not allow lagging; indeed, it does not involve extending credit to the importer at all.

The method of settlement that has not so far been mentioned is *consignment*. This method specifies that payment will be made when all the goods have been sold by the importer. Since this gives the exporter almost no control over when he receives payment, and since there is no formal document or other guarantee of full settlement, Grassman treated this as a special case of open account. There is, however, a crucial difference between consignment and open account, in that the former does not offer any flexibility to the importer as to when he pays.[4] For this reason we do not follow Grassman completely. We do classify consignment with open account when testing the hypothesis which was based upon the extent of mutual trust between traders but it is classified with the other methods of settlement when testing the hypothesis based upon the flexibility of payment allowed by different methods of settlement.

The above considerations lead to the following grouping of methods of settlement for the purposes of the statistical tests.

Group I

Open account
Regular settlement on open account
Consignment (for Hypothesis VIIB only)

Group II

Cash on delivery
Cash against documents
Payment of bills against documents
Acceptance of bills against documents
Sight documentary credits
Time documentary credits
Payment in advance
Payment by instalments
Consignment (except for Hypothesis VIIB)

Table 5.2 presents our results on the methods of settlement, classified into Groups I and II, utilised in various types of transactions. We distinguish between exports and imports, intra-MNC and other transactions, and between those invoiced in the exporter's currency and in some other currency. The first column shows the percentage of the *value* of transactions settled using flexible (Group I) methods, while the second shows the percentage of the *number* of transactions using a flexible method. The final two columns show the absolute figures underlying the second column (e.g. 67 of the 89 transactions in row 1, or 75.3%, fell in Group I), and are the figures on which the significance tests were based.

Hypothesis VII(a) 'Sales on open account or similar terms (i.e. Group I above), other than within an MNC, will be more common (a) for transactions invoiced in the exporter's currency...'

Since this hypothesis deals with non-intra MNC trade, the relevant comparisons are between rows 4 and 5, and rows 10 and 11, of Table 5.2. The hypothesis predicts that Group I will be more common for transactions invoiced in the exporter's currency than for those invoiced in other currencies. Inspection of Table 5.2 shows that this is true for imports but not for exports. A *chi*-square test revealed that this difference was significant at the one per cent level for imports (*chi*-square of 15.39 as against a critical value of 6.64), but not for exports (*chi*-square of 5.59).[5] The hypothesis therefore receives support on the import side but not in relation to exports. If the exporter is largely responsible for choice of the method of settlement and currency of invoice, as seems to be normal

Table 5.2. *Methods of settlement, classified by flexibility, used in various circumstances*

Row no.	Circumstances	Percentage of Group I by value (1)	Percentage of Group I by no. of transactions (2)	Number of transactions Grp. I (3)	Grp. II (4)
Exports					
Intra-MNC:					
1	invoiced in exporter's currency	20.7	75.3	67	22
2	invoiced in other currency	83.9	73.9	17	6
3	Total	49.2	75.0	84	23
	Between independent firms:				
4	invoiced in exporter's currency	20.0	40.1	393	588
5	invoiced in other currency	27.3	57.2	91	68
6	Total	21.3	42.5	484	656
Imports					
	Intra-MNC:				
7	invoiced in exporter's currency	84.4	77.4	72	21
8	invoiced in other currency	63.8	64.1	41	23
9	Total	75.1	72.0	113	44
	Between independent firms:				
10	invoiced in exporter's currency	24.8	50.6	243	237
11	invoiced in other currency	17.7	17.4	46	218
12	Total	21.2	38.8	289	455

Note: Consignment is classified as group II in this table.
Source: Questionnaire survey

practice, one seems bound to draw the depressing inference that foreign traders in general act rationally but British ones do not.

Hypothesis VII (*b*) 'Sales on open account or similar terms, other than within an MNC, will be more common... (b) the longer the two parties to the transaction have been trading with one another.'

Respondents to our questionnaire were divided into three groups by mutual trading experience, according to whether they had been trading less than two years, two to five years, or over five years, with their trading partner. Table 5.3 displays the data for non-intra MNC transac-

Table 5.3. *Percentage of settlement terms without formal documents*

	Length of mutual trading experience (years)		
	0–2	2–5	over 5
Exports:			
percentage by value	6.8	27.2	26.4
percentage by number of transactions	24.9	42.6	47.1
Imports:			
percentage by value	7.5	21.4	25.1
percentage by number of transactions	32.8	38.0	40.9
Memorandum item			
Number of transactions:			
exports	169	289	682
imports	67	137	540

Source: Questionnaire survey

tions, showing the percentage of transactions between partners with different lengths of mutual trading experience that were settled without the use of formal documents. These informal methods were classified as open account, regular payments on open account, and consignment, which is included as an informal method for the purpose of this test since, as noted above, it requires the seller to have considerable trust in the buyer.

It can be seen that there is indeed a tendency for use of informal methods to increase with length of mutual trading experience. As seems very reasonable, this effect is markedly more pronounced in the value figures than in those by number of transactions: where the values involved are sufficiently small, presumably the advantages of reduced invoicing costs are deemed to outweigh the additional risk of informal methods even when the basis for confidence in the partner is relatively slight. Furthermore, the figures suggest quite strongly that the process of building up trust in the partner is largely completed within two years, for the excess of the final column over the middle column is in all four cases much smaller than the difference between the first two columns, and in one case – that of exports by value – the final figure is actually slightly lower.

As usual, a *chi*-square test was applied to test whether the differences on the basis of the number of transactions were statistically significant. The values of *chi*-square are 27.33 for exports and 1.83 for imports, as against critical values of 9.21 at the one per cent level and 5.99 at the five per cent confidence level (with two degrees of freedom). The hypothesis therefore receives strong support from the export data but is not confirmed by the import data. However, in view of the much sharper differences in the figures on the basis of the value rather than the number of transactions, we feel that it is entirely reasonable to treat this hypothesis as supported by our results.

Hypothesis VIII 'All transactions within an MNC will be settled on open account.'

Taken literally, this hypothesis implies that the entries in the first two columns in rows 3 and 9 of Table 5.2 should be 100%. In this strong form the hypothesis is obviously refuted. In a weaker version, however, one may interpret the hypothesis to mean that MNCs will use flexible credit terms to a significantly greater extent than is general practice in transactions between independent firms. That they do so can readily be seen by comparing row 3 with row 6 and row 9 with row 12 in Table 5.2. A *chi*-square test was applied to the figures in these rows and the final two columns of the table to establish whether the differences are statistically significant; they are indeed, as the results reported in Table 5.4 show. It is particularly interesting to examine whether MNCs use flexible credit terms in internal transactions to a greater extent than in other cases when the invoice currency is not that of the exporter, since this is the circumstance in which theory suggests that firms selling to an independent firm will avoid the use of flexible terms because of the additional risk involved. To do this, one compares rows 2 and 5, and rows 8 and 11, of Table 5.2. It can be seen that intra-MNC transactions still use flexible settlement methods more heavily, as predicted. This difference is significant at the one per cent level on the import side, but not on the export side (Table 5.4). It seems legitimate to conclude that in its weak version this hypothesis receives strong support.

Can one infer anything from these results as to whether local branches of MNCs seek to maximise the profits of the group as a whole rather than of their particular branch? The hypothesis was formulated on the basis of the supposition that the actions of branches of MNCs would be designed to maximise the welfare of the MNC as a whole, and the success in confirming the hypothesis is therefore certainly consistent with the view that local branches of MNCs are not simply concerned with their own success regardless of that of the rest of the group (as more than one of our interviewees assured us they were). On the other hand, this evidence is not in itself conclusive, because it is conceivable that the greater willingness to use open account in intra-MNC transactions

Table 5.4. *Tests of Hypothesis VIII (weak version)*

Comparison between rows of Table 5.2	Actual *chi*-square	Critical *chi*-square
3 and 6	43.58	6.64
9 and 12	57.59	6.64
2 and 5	3.66	6.64
8 and 11	56.47	6.64

Source: Table 5.2

reflected primarily, or entirely, a high degree of trust between the branches of an MNC, rather than indifference to *where* the MNC's profits are earned. In fact the rejection of the strong version of Hypothesis VIII must be taken as evidence that such indifference is not complete. But it should also be remembered that in Section 4.2 we found evidence to support Hypothesis III (that MNCs were less likely to use exporter-currency invoicing for tradables I than were traders in general), and there is no obvious way to explain away that finding other than to accept that local branches of MNCs do take a wider view of their objectives than simply that of their own profits. We therefore offer the tentative conclusion that in general the local branches of MNCs tend to put their own success first, but to take some account of the wider interests of the group to which they belong.

5.2 Periods of credit

Average periods of credit are set out by various classifications in Table 5.5 (for exports) and Table 5.6 (for imports).[6] The various period of credit concepts used in these two tables are explained in detail in Chapter 1, pp. 8–9. It is, however, worth repeating here that concept *E*, the contract period, is different in kind from the other columns, in that it is in no respect a measure of the time for which credit is extended to the buyer by the seller. Rather, it is a measure of the time which elapsed from signing of the contract to the time when final payment was made, and is thus a measure of the time for which there was potential exposure to exchange risk for the seller, the buyer, or possibly both.

Exports As might be expected, the number of days recorded under concept *E* is larger than in any other column for all classifications in Table 5.5. It is worth noting that the average overall contract period is very close to six months, after which period forward market activity diminishes fairly sharply. This figure may therefore help provide an explanation for the fairly limited maturity of forward markets: demand for markets of much longer maturity than six months may not be large. (Contract periods by most of the categories of Table 5.5 are quite close to that overall average. The only one which is notably different is the 414 days for exports of large capital goods.)

The contract period is also important in providing a measure of how quickly foreign currency receipts can be expected to respond to an exchange rate change. Indeed, the figure for the contract period is the very *minimum* time which must elapse before currency flows can respond to an exchange rate change, in that it starts from the moment contracts are signed and continues until the transaction is completed.

Thus it seems quite clear that a lagged effect is to be expected after an exchange rate change. The implications of the length of the contract

Table 5.5. *Average periods of credit, exports (days)*

Coverage	Term of payment (*A*)	Credit term (*B*)	Credit term (revised concept) (*C*)	Credit period (*D*)	Contract period (*E*)	Sample size[a]
A *Overall:*						
By number of transactions	41.1	50.1	41.4	57.9	173.6	1,252
By value	63.1	66.5	59.9	82.3	307.1	£16,404,423
B *By trading partner:*						
Germany and Switzerland	43.4	48.3	43.3	48.7	160.6	93
Ireland and Channel Islands	45.3	45.2	41.0	47.5	118.2	44
Rest of EEC	47.2	61.3	55.4	62.9	163.4	224
Rest of Western Europe	39.9	48.7	40.8	52.5	159.6	249
Eastern Europe and USSR	−15.7	11.2	4.6	24.5	175.7	22
Developed Sterling Area	53.1	57.4	44.7	67.0	181.4	123
USA	40.1	46.2	40.2	51.7	166.4	66
Canada	50.3	65.0	57.5	72.2	197.1	46
Latin America	68.7	82.9	74.3	96.4	291.5	45
Middle East	17.1	27.0	14.7	42.3	165.8	155
Africa, south of Sahara, excluding S. Africa	52.7	68.1	48.5	79.9	175.9	48
Hong Kong and Japan	32.8	38.1	30.0	45.2	152.2	25
Rest of world	41.0	44.0	34.0	66.0	209.8	112
C *By commodity:*						
SITC 0–1	32.5	37.5	30.5	50.7	95.2	107
SITC 2 and 4	32.4	36.9	30.4	41.5	113.4	50
SITC 3	67.3	64.9	59.0	70.7	178.0	13
SITC 5	51.0	56.6	46.7	67.2	128.0	132
SITC 6	44.6	57.1	46.8	62.4	160.1	376
SITC 71–2 excluding large capital goods	28.7	39.1	32.6	47.8	220.7	295
SITC 73 excluding ships	32.8	45.4	35.1	51.5	210.8	72
SITC 8	50.3	57.0	46.8	64.1	177.5	185
Large capital goods	84.1	83.9	80.7	104.9	413.7	22

All commodities excluding large capital goods	40.3	49.6	40.7	57.2	169.5	1,230
Tradables I	41.7	51.4	42.4	58.9	183.1	1,025
Tradables II	38.0	44.4	37.0	53.4	130.7	227
Tradables I excluding large capital goods	40.9	50.7	41.6	58.1	178.3	1,003
D *By affiliation:*						
Between independent companies	35.7	46.1	37.1	54.2	171.4	1,140
Intra-MNC	95.9	90.7	85.4	95.3	197.3	112
E *By size of transaction:*						
Bottom 60%	42.7	52.4	43.7	59.2	154.7	751
Next 30%	38.9	46.9	37.5	54.9	173.5	376
Top 10%	37.7	45.9	38.7	58.9	285.5	125
F *By currency:*						
Sterling (i.e. sellers)	39.3	48.3	39.3	56.6	172.6	1,070
Buyers	51.6	60.0	55.0	64.1	168.6	142
US $ as 3rd	55.3	64.1	57.7	70.9	226.6	30
Other 3rds	39.2	64.9	21.1	73.2	198.4	10
G *By method of settlement:*						
Open account	57.0	65.1	57.2	65.7	164.4	494
Periodic settlement	58.7	61.2	58.1	64.9	177.6	74
Cash on delivery	9.5	22.8	9.8	34.4	128.0	31
Cash against documents	6.1	25.0	12.5	39.9	143.7	173
Payment of bills against documents	–	8.7	−2.3	39.9	146.4	54
Sight documentary credits	–	2.9	−3.3	24.0	179.8	132
Acceptance of bills against documents	84.5	93.7	83.1	100.1	220.2	207
Time documentary credits	86.7	98.3	81.1	103.0	184.3	32
Advance (whole amount)	−17.1	−17.0	−17.1	−13.9	18.0	15
Advance (prior to instalments)	−289.7	−289.7	−290.5	−291.4	102.2	23
Instalments	258.1	300.1	296.7	300.3	521.9	15
Consignment	180.0	...	...	...	270.0	2

Notes:
[a] The sample size is the maximum possible; individual columns may vary slightly as a result of non-response
... Signifies no responses
Source: Questionnaire survey

period for the existence and length of the J-curve are further discussed in Section 6.1.2.

Looking next at the various concepts of the period of credit (concepts *A* to *D*) one observes that overall (Section A) the credit period exceeds the credit term (revised concept), and the credit term exceeds the term of payment. In discussing these differences, it is useful to look at various breakdowns of the overall findings.

The credit period is the time between registration of the goods at Customs and payment being received by the exporter; the credit term (revised concept) is the period which elapses between receipt (i.e. formal acceptance or delivery) of the goods and payment being made. The difference between the two consists of (a) the gap between registration with UK Customs and the date of delivery, and (b) delays in remission of payment by the banks. For exports, the first element includes transit time from the UK port to the importing country; accordingly the differences between columns C and D are substantial. (Most of the figures in the classifications of periods of credit by trading partner suggest that transit time is the dominant element. The implied transit times from the UK are six days to other European countries, twelve days to North America, fifteen days to Japan, and thirty days for most non-OECD destinations, which seems plausible except for Japan.) Delays in remission of payment can however occasionally be significant.

The credit period is in itself an important figure. When goods are registered at customs they are entered in the trade accounts as measured on a 'transactions basis'. However, the shipping of goods does not have any effect on the exchange market until payment is actually made, at which time the record is in principle entered in the payments accounts as measured on a 'balance of payments basis'. The credit period is a measure of the gap between these two bases for trade statistics.

Looking at the other columns as broken down by trading partner, the most conspicuous figure is the negative entry under the term of payment for Eastern Europe and the USSR. Term of payment is the period of credit specified in the contract, and the negative entry therefore indicates that payment in advance is in general required from these countries.

There is in general some excess of the credit term (which is defined as the 'ex post' version of concept *A* – that is, the time from when the credit term actually starts to when payment is made) over the term of payment. This is due not only to delays in making payment, but also to the time which elapses between payment being made and received. The occasional substantial discrepancy was ascribed by several firms with which we raised this matter to slow banking practices in certain countries, and slowness in converting some currencies to sterling.

Consider next the classification by commodity group (Section C). Among the contract period data, outstanding is the 414 days for large capital goods. This is of course not surprising, such goods often being made to order and needing a long period of production. Column *D* here again consistently exceeds Column *C*, with the excess, ascribed above to period of transportation, being in the range of ten to about twenty days.

What is striking when one looks at periods of credit as broken down by tradables category is the *lack* of contrast. By any concept, periods of credit are shorter for tradables II than for tradables I, but, with the exception of the contract period, the largest difference is seven days as between credit terms. These differences narrow further when large capital goods are removed from tradables I. Within the tradables categories, the usual pattern can be seen; the contract period is longer than any other period of credit, the credit period exceeds the credit term-revised concept, and the credit term exceeds the term of payment.

Looking at periods of credit classified by affiliation (Section D) there is a striking contrast between trade between independent companies and trade within an MNC. The contract period is a little longer for the latter, but, for all measures of the period of credit, the period for intra-MNC trade is twice as long or longer than it is for trade between independent companies. Furthermore, for intra-MNC trade the credit term is *shorter* than the term of payment, in contrast to the general pattern. Since one hardly expects banking delays to have a different effect on intra-MNC and other transactions, one may conclude that MNCs differ in normally settling their internal transactions somewhat before the due date. In short, branches normally allow each other more credit, but they typically do not use it all; which clearly leaves them scope to use more or less when circumstances so warrant.

No distinctive pattern seems to emerge when one looks at periods of credit classified by size of transaction (Section E). The one outstanding observation is the contract period for the top 10% of transactions by size; not surprisingly, those often being large capital goods produced to special order, this contract period is much longer than that for the other two categories of transaction size.

The next breakdown provided is of periods of credit by currency of invoice (Section F). The relationships which have occurred with sufficient regularity to be described as 'usual' hold here also. The contract period (Column *E*) is substantially larger than any measure of the period of credit, the credit period exceeds the credit term (revised concept), and the credit term exceeds the term of payment. Nonetheless, this table does contain some surprises. The longest contract periods are when third currencies (the US dollar or some other) are used. By every measure of length of credit granted from seller to buyer, this is shortest when the invoice is in sterling.

Looking finally, for exports, at periods of credit as broken down by methods of settlement (Section G), we find that these conform to expectation; that is to say, periods of credit are longest when a document

Table 5.6. *Average periods of credit, imports (days)*

Coverage	Term of payment (*A*)	Credit term (*B*)	Credit term (revised concept) (*C*)	Credit period (*D*)	Contract period (*E*)	Sample size[a]
A *Overall:*						
By number of transactions	45.9	48.4	42.9	42.6	135.0	901
By value	41.8	43.4	38.8	37.5	116.1	£13,907,639
B *By trading partner:*						
Germany and Switzerland	49.2	56.9	52.3	54.6	139.6	163
Rest of EEC	54.6	54.5	49.1	50.4	114.0	219
Rest of Western Europe	45.0	48.8	44.1	45.1	141.9	125
Eastern Europe and USSR	35.2	40.9	40.0	38.9	196.7	30
Developed Sterling Area	31.3	22.3	18.5	18.5	105.1	36
USA	52.7	66.0	57.9	57.6	153.8	107
Canada	54.1	57.0	51.7	51.3	146.4	23
Latin America	10.1	9.0	7.9	4.8	88.4	17
Middle East	9.3	11.3	8.4	4.3	94.1	12
Africa, south of Sahara, excluding S. Africa	13.6	12.8	10.8	10.0	141.7	11
Hong Kong and Japan	54.2	46.0	35.6	37.1	159.3	80
Rest of world	24.7	22.5	19.3	6.3	123.8	78
C *By commodity:*						
SITC 0–1	39.6	34.8	32.0	30.1	102.6	142
SITC 2 and 4	22.5	21.0	17.2	15.6	125.8	129
SITC 3	19.8	22.8	22.8	23.0	77.8	5
SITC 5	52.4	67.0	59.6	59.9	110.5	70
SITC 6	47.8	46.8	41.0	40.9	133.5	218
SITC 71/2	53.8	64.6	58.2	59.7	161.3	162
SITC 73	45.8	57.9	50.0	46.9	172.1	21

SITC 8	58.2	60.2	53.5	53.2	154.9	154
Tradables I	53.4	58.1	51.8	51.8	145.1	601
Tradables II	30.9	28.9	25.3	24.3	114.9	300
D *By affiliation:*						
Between independent companies	38.8	41.1	36.0	35.3	129.5	744
Intra-MNC	79.7	83.1	76.0	77.1	160.6	157
E *By size of transaction:*						
Bottom 60%	46.6	48.9	42.9	42.8	131.8	541
Next 30%	43.0	46.5	42.3	41.0	138.3	270
Top 10%	50.3	50.5	45.0	46.1	143.8	90
F *By currency:*						
Sterling (i.e. buyers)	40.8	37.7	33.6	32.5	124.9	254
Sellers	50.1	54.6	48.4	48.6	142.3	573
US $ as 3rd	29.6	33.2	29.1	26.9	102.3	61
Other 3rds	36.9	52.8	52.8	49.4	164.2	13
G *By method of settlement:*						
Open account	62.9	70.8	62.2	64.4	138.8	344
Periodic settlement	66.0	58.5	56.3	57.6	158.0	58
Cash on delivery	7.0	19.8	20.4	21.3	107.4	59
Cash against documents	1.2	3.3	3.1	2.7	108.8	159
Payment of bills against documents	–	10.8	10.8	8.2	72.9	18
Sight documentary credits	–	−1.5	−4.5	−12.3	108.1	57
Acceptance of bills against documents	77.3	73.7	65.5	63.1	166.2	121
Time documentary credits	80.7	76.9	69.4	63.7	179.3	61
Advance (whole amount)	−31.8	−31.8	−31.8	−30.0	39.8	4
Advance (prior to instalments)	−84.9	−82.3	−81.7	−84.9	52.3	7
Instalments	127.0	131.0	131.0	136.6	208.8	5
Consignment	138.8	66.1	66.1	70.4	121.8	8

Notes:
[a] The sample size is the maximum possible; individual columns may vary slightly as a result of non-response
Source: Questionnaire Survey.

which explicitly grants credit is used. After instalments, the methods that exhibit the longest periods of credit are acceptance of bills against documents and time documentary credits. It is worth noting, though, that periods of credit are fairly lengthy on both open account and periodic settlements on open account. The difference in periods of credit between these two themselves is negligible.[7] With the predictable exception of instalments, contract periods do not display great variation by methods of settlement.

Imports We next consider average periods of credit for UK imports. These are displayed in Table 5.6 in the same categories as were exports in Table 5.5. As was the case with exports, the contract period is substantially larger than any measure of the period of credit, and is certainly long enough to contribute to a J-curve should the invoicing currency be appropriate. Here, too, the contract period is less than six months, adding weight to the conjecture that a reason for forward markets thinning so rapidly beyond that point is lack of demand. When one looks at the measures of periods of credit, however, some differences from what was found in our export data start to emerge.

The difference between the credit period and the credit term (revised concept) consists of (a) the difference between the date of registration with HM Customs and the date of delivery, and (b) delays in remission of payments by the banks. In the case of exports, the first element includes transit time from the UK port to the importing country and is thus a major factor; accordingly the differences between columns *C* and *D* are substantial. Delays in remission of payments may also be significant. Imports, however, have at most to travel from UK customs to their British recipient, so there is no reason on this account to expect a significant gap between these two measures of the period of credit. Furthermore, factor (b) does not arise on the import side. Reassuringly, the two measures are very similar almost throughout the table.

The credit term is still slightly longer than the term of payment, but the difference is much reduced as compared with the result for exports. Again, this is to be expected, since delays in the remission of funds would not be included in the credit term for imports as they are for exports. The fact that a payment is not remitted within the term of payment as we have defined it does not, perhaps confusingly, necessarily imply that the importer has fallen down on his obligations. It may also be due to factors such as late delivery, late presentation of documents, etc.

Looking at the results in Section B, it can be seen that the overal result that the credit period is shorter for imports than for exports is valid for all areas except Germany and Switzerland, the USA, and Eastern Europe and the USSR. This last case is presumably a reflection of the reluctance of British exporters to extend credit to the communist countries on which we commented previously (a reluctance which is clearly not reciprocated). The other two exceptions are rather interesting, representing as they do the two areas whose currencies have an extensive international role. It is well known that, when London was the financial capital of the world, Britain used to provide the credit to finance her imports as well as her exports. To examine whether a similar phenomenon can be detected in our statistics, we calculated the *differences* between the two principal measures of the period of credit on exports and on imports. The results are shown in Table 5.7.

It can be seen that, apart from the exception of Eastern Europe and the USSR already noted, there is indeed a rough correspondence between the financial strength of an area and whether it tended to grant more credit to Britain than it received (negative entries in the table) or *vice versa* (positive entries). The other developed countries generally offered the UK slightly more extensive terms of payment than they typically received from her (although only for Germany, Switzerland and the USA was this sufficient to outweigh the asymmetry of transit times incorporated in the credit period). In contrast, the underdeveloped countries received longer terms of payment than they granted; although this effect was, plausibly enough, smaller for the liquid Middle East than for the other, cash-short, developing areas. As in the 'hierarchy of currencies' (Section 4.1), the Developed Sterling Area appears somewhat financially underdeveloped – or, in this case, perhaps just capital-short.

Section C of Table 5.6 shows very clearly that periods of credit for raw materials, fuels, and to a lesser extent food are substantially shorter than

Table 5.7. *Excess of average periods of credit for exports over imports* (days)

Area	Term of payment (*A*)	Credit period (*D*)
Germany and Switzerland	– 5.8	– 5.9
Rest of EEC	– 7.4	12.5
Rest of Western Europe	– 5.1	7.4
Eastern Europe and USSR	–50.9	–14.4
Developed Sterling Area	21.8	48.5
USA	–12.6	– 5.9
Canada	– 3.8	20.9
Latin America	58.6	91.6
Middle East	7.8	38.0
Africa south of Sahara excluding S. Africa	39.1	69.9
Hong Kong and Japan	–21.4	8.1
Rest of the world	16.3	59.7
Mean for all areas	– 4.8	15.3

Source: Tables 5.5 and 5.6

those for manufactures. Since these are the principal exports of the underdeveloped areas to Britain, this might explain, at least in part, the longer credits granted to these countries over those received from them. The fact that terms of payment for most SITC categories are marginally longer on the import side than on the export side suggests, however, that the geographical differences noted in Table 5.7 are *not* simply a reflection of these differences in the composition of trade.

Disaggregating periods of credit by affiliation (Section D) reveals exactly the same pattern for imports as it did for exports; that is, every measure of the period of credit is twice or more as long for intra-MNC transactions as it is for transactions between independent companies. This finding is therefore consistent with our previous tentative conclusion that MNCs have some concern for the profits of the whole firm rather than just their individual branch. The findings also suggest that, since the gap between periods of credit between independent companies is shorter than that for intra-MNC trade for both imports and exports, at least in our data period MNCs were not using variations in credit either to bring funds in to the UK or to take them out.

As was found with exports, size of transaction has no particular influence on periods of credit (Section E). Indeed, it does not even boost the contract period in the top 10 per cent of transactions as was found with exports. This may reflect the differing compositions of exports and imports, and in particular the absence of large capital goods from our import sample.

The breakdown of periods of credit by invoice currency (Section F) does not reveal any striking results. Contract periods are longest when 'other' third currencies are involved, whereas on the export side the longest average contract period was associated with the use of the dollar as a third currency. Since this had the shortest contract period in the import sample, however, it is not clear that much significance can be attached to these differences.

Turning finally to periods of credit as classified by methods of settlement (Section G), the pattern is much as one would expect. Apart from consignment, periods of credit are longest in those methods of settlement that formally embody the grant of credit, followed remarkably closely – or even exceeded on one measure – by open account.

A number of comparisons between the results for imports and those for exports were made in the course of the preceding discussion. It is perhaps worth mentioning explicitly the degree to which the results on the two sides of the trade account run parallel. Both contract periods and periods of credit are broadly similar in length for exports and imports. The shorter periods of credit that one might expect to find in primary commodities are more evident on the import side, but a trace of the same effect can be found in the export data as well. The differences between intra-MNC and other transactions are striking, and strikingly similar between exports and imports. In neither case does the size of transaction play any systematic role in influencing periods of credit. And in both cases acceptance bills and time documentary credits provide the longest periods of credit, followed quite closely by open account. The data do, it seems, exhibit regularities.

6

IMPLICATIONS FOR THE FOREIGN EXCHANGE MARKET

We are now in a position to move on from the presentation and analysis of our results to a consideration of their implications. The present chapter deals with their implications for the behaviour of the foreign exchange market, while the next one turns to policy implications.

It is convenient to divide the discussion of the implications of trade financing practices for the foreign exchange market into three parts. In the first section of the chapter we therefore consider the implications of the choice of invoice currency under capital immobility. In the second section we consider the implications of prevailing credit practices for capital mobility, by endeavouring to provide some quantification of the scope for leads and lags. In the final section we seek to bring the two strands of analysis together.

6.1 The choice of invoice currency with capital immobility

In the absence of commercial credit one can define capital immobility rather naturally as a situation where the only exchanges of financial assets between the residents of different countries are those that arise out of the process of settling current account transactions. However, when goods are not automatically paid for immediately on delivery – i.e. when commercial credit is present – this definition is inadequate, since the essence of capital movements through variations in commercial credit consists of changes in the *date* on which payment for goods being exchanged in trade is made. There are two ways that one might think of extending the definition of capital immobility to take account of the complications posed by the existence of commercial credits, but unfortunately neither of these is completely satisfactory in general. One way is to require that total net commercial credit outstanding be constant. The problem with this definition is that the value of net commercial credit outstanding can change without anything that one would want to call a capital movement occurring. For example, an exchange rate change must necessarily alter the net value of commercial credit outstanding as measured in at least one of the two currencies involved. An alternative approach would be to require that the period of credit involved in financing trade transactions be constant. The problem with this definition is that it denies that an export of capital takes place when more trade credit is given to the rest of the world as a result of a rise in exports with the same period of credit as that on existing exports. This is a pretty devastating objection to the general use of this definition, but it is not important in the present context and we shall therefore identify capital immobility with a situation in which the only transactions in the foreign exchange market are those needed to make current account payments, and all of these payments are made at a predetermined time after delivery of the goods or services in question.

In these circumstances, the demand and supply of foreign exchange on a particular day are determined by the contracts whose periods of credit expire on that day. If contracts are denominated in the domestic currency of the exporter, it is the importers who come to the foreign exchange market in order to acquire the exporter's currency. If contracts are denominated in the importer's currency, the exporters receive payment in foreign currency and place this supply on the market.[1] In either event, importers come to the market with a demand, or exporters with a supply, that is predetermined in terms of the currency of invoice. Under these circumstances the currency of invoice can be a matter of great consequence. We analyse below what those consequences are under the five distinct types of exchange rate regime.

6.1.1 *Free floating*

Consider first the case where the exchange rate is allowed to float freely with no intervention at all by the central bank. If contracts are denominated in the currency of the exporter, a depreciation of the domestic currency will reduce the foreign-currency value of the predetermined volume of exports being paid for at a pre-determined domestic-currency price, while leaving the foreign-currency value of import payments unchanged. Since export payments provide the supply of foreign exchange while import payments provide the demand, the supply of foreign exchange will fall relative to the demand, i.e. the excess demand for foreign exchange will increase. This will intensify the depreciation. If, on the other hand, contracts are denominated in the currency of the importer, a depreciation of the domestic currency will leave the foreign-currency value of exports unchanged, while reducing the foreign-currency value of imports, thus reducing the excess demand for foreign exchange and relieving the pressure for depreciation.

This simple but important result may be stated formally as a theorem and proved.

Theorem. With zero capital mobility, a freely-floating exchange rate would be globally unstable if all trade contracts were denominated in the exporter's currency, and globally stable if all trade contracts were denominated in the importer's currency.

Proof. Let x = value of exports due for settlement in currency of denomination.
X = value of exports due for settlement in foreign currency.
m = value of imports due for settlement in currency of denomination.
M = value of imports due for settlement in foreign currency.
r = exchange rate (units of foreign exchange/unit of domestic currency).

Postulate that the exchange rate appreciates when there is excess supply of foreign exchange, i.e.

$$\dot{r} = \alpha(X - M)$$

Case A. All contracts are denominated in the exporter's currency.

Then $X = xr, \qquad M = m$

so $\dot{r} = \alpha(xr - m)$

and $\dfrac{\partial \dot{r}}{\partial r} = \alpha x > 0$, i.e. the exchange rate is unstable

Case B. All contracts are denominated in the importer's currency.

Then $X = x \qquad M = mr$

so $\dot{r} = \alpha(x - mr)$

and $\dfrac{\partial \dot{r}}{\partial r} = -\alpha m < 0$, i.e. the exchange rate is stable

The evidence indicates quite decisively that in Britain, as in the other industrial countries, exports are denominated predominantly in domestic currency, while imports are denominated predominantly in foreign currency. One can therefore conclude that, in the absence of capital mobility or central bank intervention, the foreign exchange market would be dynamically unstable. This instability is global; it is not a case of an unstable equilibrium being surrounded by two stable equilibria, as in the traditional analysis of the 'static instability' of the foreign exchange market (Kemp, 1964, Ch. 13). The fact that the market would be unstable without capital mobility or central bank intervention is in no way inconsistent with the presence of stabilising responses of trade volumes to exchange rate changes in the long run, i.e. with the Marshall–Lerner condition being satisfied. What the latter implies is that a depreciation or appreciation that originated because of a trade deficit or surplus, but was limited in extent by speculation or intervention, would ultimately generate trade changes that would tend to eliminate the initial cause of disequilibrium. What the present theorem says is that without the speculation or intervention one would have no chance to observe what would happen in the long run because the market would explode to an exchange rate of zero or infinity in the short run.

In the preceding analysis we have abstracted from the possibility that transactions are covered in the forward market. This abstraction is in fact entirely natural so long as one is also abstracting from capital mobility for in that event the instability of the spot exchange market is unaffected by the existence of a forward market. Some fraction of the contracts due for settlement on a date 't' are settled at a rate that has been determined at some previous time(s). Importers who have covered forward receive their foreign exchange from foreign importers who have also covered forward at a rate that in general differs from the spot rate. But, on the assumption of zero capital mobility, the values of trade transactions whose forward contracts mature on a date t must be balanced. Hence introduction of the forward market cannot alter the conclusion that the foreign exchange market is unstable when capital is immobile and trade contracts are denominated in the exporters' currency. Its introduction does, however, have interesting implications, at least in principle, in the presence of capital mobility. These will be noted subsequently.

6.1.2 *The adjustable peg*

The same pattern of invoicing practices that implies the dynamic instability of a freely floating exchange rate under capital immobility also makes probable the existence of a short-run J-curve following the devaluation of a pegged exchange rate. With export contracts denominated in domestic currency and import contracts in foreign currency, devaluation of the domestic currency implies that export receipts measured in foreign currency must fall, while import payments similarly measured in foreign currency must remain constant (both as compared to what they would otherwise have been), for some period following the devaluation. This must, in fact, remain true at least until contracts signed after the devaluation start to fall due for settlement. We term this the 'invoice effect'.

The invoice effect is only one of three effects that jointly determine the shape of the J-curve. The second effect involves the changes in the prices of exports and imports that will be incorporated in newly-signed contracts as firms adjust their prices so as to optimise in the new circumstances confronting them. The third effect is of course the response of trade volumes to these changes in relative prices.

It is possible to give a schematic representation of these three effects

(Figure 6.1). Assume that the time profile of all trade contracts were identical, so that the three effects can be identified with three distinct phases of the J-curve. Devaluation occurs at t_0. From then until t_1, the invoice effect operates: previously-negotiated contracts are settled at rates which involve lower net foreign currency earnings. At t_1, the new prices announced by traders at t_0 are first reflected in invoices coming due for settlement, but, because of inertia in ordering habits, trade volumes still do not adjust. Since any price adjustments that domestic exporters may find it advantageous to make will certainly be upward in terms of domestic currency (although downward in terms of foreign currency in comparison to the pre-devaluation situation), while any that foreign exporters may make will certainly be downward in terms of their own currency (although upward in terms of the depreciated currency in comparison to the pre-devaluation level), the trade balance will certainly improve during this second phase as compared to the first phase when the invoice effect was operating. However, granted the normal pre-

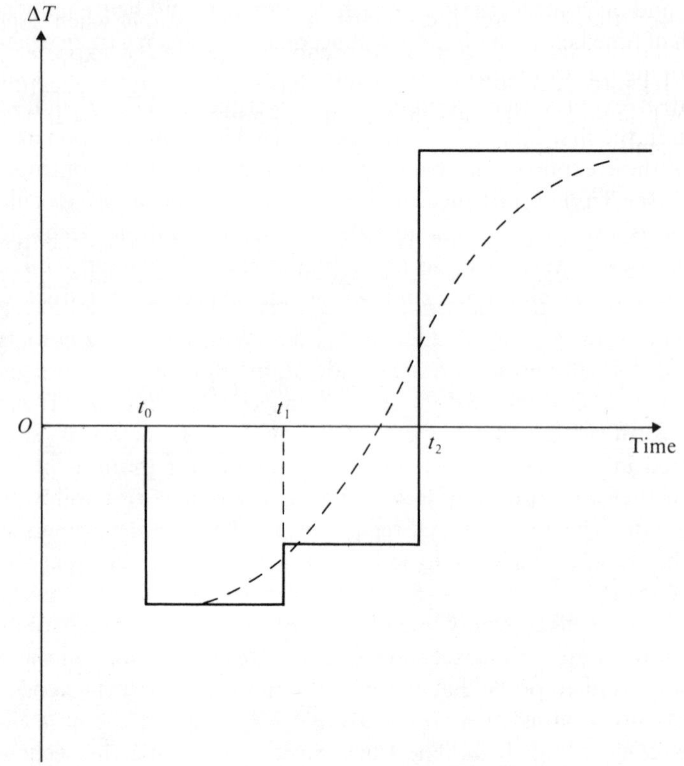

Figure 6.1 A stylised J-curve
ΔT=change in trade balance (measured in foreign currency) from no-devaluation situation

sumption that exporters find it advantageous to make bigger cuts in foreign currency prices in response to a devaluation than the cuts in their own currency prices that foreign exporters will choose to make (a presumption motivated by the asymmetrical cost situations), the J-curve will still be negative in the second phase between t_1 and t_2. It is only when the volume responses to the price changes induced by devaluation come into effect at t_2 that there is a presumption that the trade balance will improve in comparison to the no-devaluation situation, i.e. that the J-curve will become positive. The sufficient condition for this to occur is that the Marshall–Lerner condition be satisfied.

In reality, of course, the time profiles of trade contracts differ, and as a result these three phases of the J-curve overlap for different contracts, giving rise to a J-curve of the traditional J shape as indicated by the broken line in Figure 6.1. Since our survey was not designed to yield information about the relation of prices and exchange rates or the speed of response of trade volumes to price changes, we are not in a position to offer a complete estimate of the shape of the J-curve. However, we did collect information on invoicing practices, which determine the depth of the invoice effect, and on contract periods, which determine t_1 and hence influence the length of time before the J-curve can become positive. We therefore turn to developing our estimates on these topics.

British exports were running at an average of £1,589 millions per month in the first half of 1975, the period to which our data relate. Some 12% of these exports were paid for within a month of the contract being signed (see Table 6.1); hence the invoice effect would apply to only 88% of exports even in the first month after a devaluation. Some 76% of British exports were invoiced in sterling (Table 4.1, Section A). Hence a 10% sterling devaluation could have been expected to reduce export

Table 6.1. *Contract periods for UK exports and imports*

Length of contract period	Exports % by value	Imports % by value
Up to 30 days	12.1	14.9
31–60 days	5.5	12.2
61–90 days	7.3	21.6
91–120 days	6.3	19.4
121–150 days	4.2	3.9
151–180 days	4.5	12.8
181–365 days	31.5	12.2
12–21 months	20.4	2.5
More than 21 months	8.1	0.5
Average (days)	174	135

Source: Questionnaire survey

receipts in foreign currency terms by the equivalent of some £106 millions. Imports averaged £1,953 millions per month. The invoice effect only had a chance to apply to 85% of them (Table 6.1), and 30% were sterling-invoiced by our estimate (Table 4.2, Section A), so that the cost of imports in foreign currency terms might have fallen by some £50 millions. The trade balance would therefore have deteriorated by something of the order of £56 millions in the first month after a 10% sterling devaluation on account of the invoice effect. In order to permit appreciation of the magnitude of this effect, it may be useful to note that it amounts to slightly over 3% of the average value of exports and imports.

Whether the J-curve effect in total was initially larger or smaller than the invoice effect would depend upon the behaviour of the trade whose contract period expired within the first month. If most of this trade were still in the second phase of the J-curve (i.e. after price had been adjusted but before volume had responded), the value of the trade balance would fall by more than the invoice effect. The possible effect in this direction could not, however, be large: given invoicing patterns, one can put an upper limit on the negative J-curve effect simply by assuming that the invoice effect applied to all trade rather than only to that part not settled within the month. This would give an invoice effect, and total J-curve effect, of some £62 millions. If, on the other hand, there were already a volume response on a substantial part of the trade with a contract period of less than a month, the total J-curve effect could be less than the invoice effect. It is impossible from our data to place any floor on the size of the initial J-curve effect, or even to guarantee that it be negative (see next paragraph). Our guess, however, would be that our calculation of the initial value of the invoice effect probably gives a good indication of the initial depth of the J-curve.

The second topic on which our results can cast some light is the length of the negative phase of the J-curve. This in part depends upon the distribution of lengths of contract periods, on which we display our findings in Table 6.1. Rather surprisingly, it transpires that a non-negligible fraction of trade, some 12% of exports and 15% of imports, is paid for within a month of the contract being signed. This means that one cannot affirm as a matter of logical necessity that the J-curve effect will in total be negative even in the first month following a devaluation: it is in principle possible that the volume response on the 12% exports and 15% of imports for which the contract was signed in the previous month might be sufficiently great to outweigh both the invoice effect on the remaining 88 and 85% of trade and the negative price effect on the 12 and 15% themselves. This is not, of course, at all probable. The invoice effect was estimated above as some £56 millions in the first month. In order to avoid a negative J-curve effect in that month, it would be necessary for the £484 millions of trade settled within a month of the contract date (£191 millions of exports and £293 millions of imports) to show an improved balance of at least £56 millions. This would require that each depreciation of 1% produce an increase in export receipts or fall in import payments of something over 1% of the value of the affected trade. This would happen, for example, with infinite supply elasticities and elasticities of demand for exports and imports of something over two; which are the sort of assumptions that economists do in fact often use (though they are toward the top end of the range regarded as plausible). However, it is now generally accepted that the lags involved in the adjustment of trade flows to price changes are lengthy; it would typically be assumed that elasticities as high as those just cited would be evident only after at least two or three years, rather than within one month. It might of course be that the trade with the shortest contract period would tend to be that which would respond to price changes most rapidly, but it would need a very extreme case indeed for the short-run trade response to neutralise the invoice effect. Accordingly, we conclude that, while our results (assuming that they are in fact representative) do not conclusively prove that the short-run J-curve would have been negative, they leave an overwhelming presumption to that effect.

Calculations similar to that just made for the first month can be made for intervals of one month up to 6 months, and 12 and 21 months. The results are presented in Table 6.2. They show that the invoice effect remains roughly constant for the first six months, rather than starting to erode immediately as one might have expected. The reason is that the natural erosion of the invoice effect by the fall in the proportion of payments falling due which were invoiced before the devaluation is offset

Table 6.2. *Some elements of the time path of the J-curve*

Months after devaluation	Estimated invoice effect (£ millions)	Value of trade whose contract period had expired[a]		
		Exports	Imports	Total
1	−56	191	293	484
2	−57	280	529	809
3	−61	396	951	1,347
4	−63	496	1,330	1,826
5	−62	563	1,406	1,969
6	−63	634	1,656	2,290
12	−33	1,135	1,894	3,029
21	−10	1,460	1,943	3,403

Note:
[a] In millions of pounds, on the basis of the trade values prevailing in the first half of 1975
Source: Questionnaire survey results extrapolated to whole of trade

by the tendency for imports (where such invoice effect as exists tends to *improve* the trade balance) to be settled more quickly than exports. However, the proportion of trade able to respond to an exchange-rate change grows rapidly. The development of an informed judgment as to how long the negative phase of the J-curve can be expected to persist continues to require estimates of the trade elasticities, and of their time path, of the sort that econometricians have been seeking for the last quarter century. Unfortunately, we are not aware of any estimates for the UK that are sufficiently precise to allow us to combine them with the data in Table 6.2 to form a reasonable estimate of the time that must lapse before the J-curve can be expected to turn positive. We present our estimates so that others may use them in this way as and when satisfactory elasticity estimates are developed.

6.1.3 *The crawling peg*

The crawling peg is an exchange-rate regime under which any devaluation would be made in a series of small steps, rather than in the single step that occurs under the adjustable peg and whose results were studied in the previous sub-section. For example, a 10% devaluation might be undertaken in a series of steps of 1% each, spread over a period of 20 or 30 months. It has usually been assumed that the effect of doing this would be to create ten small J-curves (each of them essentially one tenth the size of the J-curve that would result from a 10% step devaluation), which would come into operation sequentially as illustrated in Figure 6.2. This would give rise to a saw-toothed overall J-curve, formed by vertical summation of the small J-curves. As compared to the magnified version of the first small J-curve that would occur under a step devaluation, the crawling peg's saw-toothed J-curve would be relatively flat and would take a longer time to show a net positive result.

This would seem to be a correct analysis of a comparison between a one-shot devaluation and the accomplishment of the same ultimate devaluation by a series of unannounced and unanticipated mini-devaluations. However, it is not clear that this is a legitimate and relevant comparison. A step devaluation cannot be announced in advance because of the speculative pressures that this would cause; hence the scope for (for example) sterling-invoicing exporters to raise their sterling prices on orders with long contract periods in anticipation of an expected sterling devaluation is bound to be very limited or non-existent. In contrast, it has been argued (e.g. Williamson, 1965) that an impending exchange-rate change that is to be made by crawling can and should be announced in advance – and this policy has in fact been applied, by Chile, during 1978. If the future path of the exchange rate were announced in advance with substantial accuracy, and these announced intentions were generally believed by traders, one would expect prices

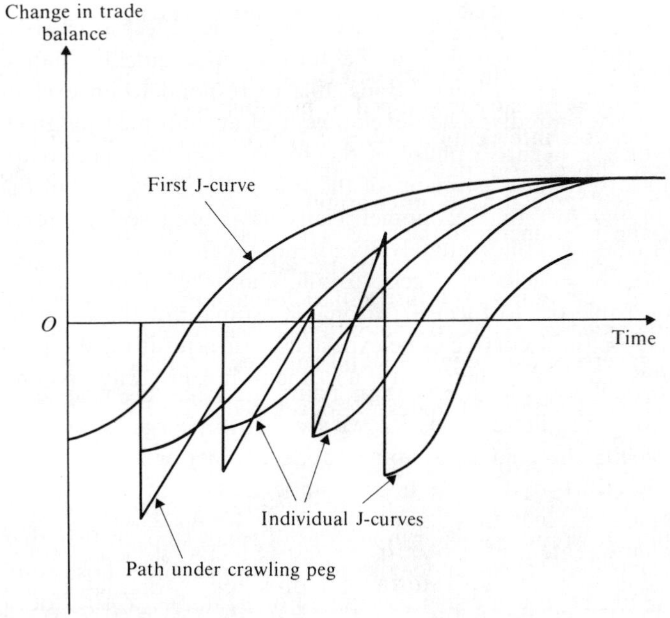

Figure 6.2 The J-curve under an unannounced crawling peg

quoted and invoiced to be adjusted to those that would be appropriate for the spot exchange rate that would prevail when the contract was due to be fulfilled. In these circumstances the invoice effect, and perhaps any negative part of the J-curve, would not exist. In effect, because of the advance notice that traders would receive of a forthcoming change in relative prices, they would be able to go out and solicit the extra business potentially available at these prices without the prior need to accept a period when prices paid by their foreign customers were low but those customers were unable to respond by placing more orders. Thus it is not at all clear that the limitation on the speed with which the exchange rate can be changed which is implied by adopting a crawling peg would involve the sacrifice of the ability to secure prompt adjustment that has sometimes been envisaged.

6.1.4 *Fixed exchange rates*

With fixed, as opposed to temporarily pegged, exchange rates, the choice of invoice currency is entirely inconsequential. This is hardly surprising: there is in effect only one currency.

6.1.5 *Managed floating*

Managed floating occurs when a central bank continues to intervene in the foreign exchange market, but without accepting any obligation to defend a particular exchange rate. There are at least three analytically distinct cases encompassed under this heading, depending upon the nature of the intervention policy pursued by the central bank. Fortunately each of these cases can be handled rather briefly by drawing on the analysis already developed in previous sections.

One possible intervention policy is that of 'leaning against the wind', in which the central bank sells (buys) reserves when the domestic currency is depreciating (appreciating), but not in sufficient quantity to reverse the movement of the rate. The analysis of free floating would seem relevant to this case. In particular, such an intervention policy would not seem able to stabilise a market that was unstable as a result of invoicing practices, since by definition it merely reduces, but does not seek to reverse, excess demands and supplies.

A second possible intervention policy that has been suggested and discussed in the literature is known as that for 'target zones' or 'target rates'. While there may be some subtle distinctions between the proposals described by these terms, the important features which they have in common are that they involve the central bank having some idea of the exchange rate that it regards as desirable and some commitment to intervening to push the rate in that direction, with that commitment increasing the greater is the deviation from the target (rate or zone). So long as the system is one of floating there cannot, by definition, be any point at which that commitment becomes absolute. Nevertheless, there would seem to be a presumption that a sufficiently vigorous policy of this character would stabilise an otherwise-unstable market. It may be noted that the 'reference rate proposal' for the management of floating rates would permit, though it would not compel, this type of strategy.

A third possible type of intervention policy, which has not to our knowledge been recommended in the literature but has certainly been applied in practice, for example by the Bank of England and the Bank of Japan, may be termed 'the unannounced, adjustable-under-pressure peg'. This policy involves stabilising the rate until strong market pressures develop, and then more or less withdrawing from the market until things quieten down to the point where it is possible to stabilise some other rate. In the periods when the rate is floating, it floats relatively freely, and hence the stability problems characteristic of free floating can be expected to arise. As between two periods of stabilised rates, one may expect to find the J-curve characteristic of the adjustable peg.

6.2 Capital mobility

The second important impact of trade financing practices on the foreign exchange market arises from the implications for capital mobility. To the extent that their contract permits them to vary the payment date t_P, importers can export or import capital by a unilateral decision.

Furthermore, contract terms can be altered as new contracts are negotiated in order to export or import capital by mutual agreement between the trading partners. It has been widely known for many years that such leads and lags in commercial payments can lead to large capital movements that are virtually immune from exchange control – although, as noted in Section 2.4, surprisingly little is known in a quantitative way as to how large such capital movements can be.

We therefore turn to developing an estimate of the stock of capital that can be shifted through variations in trade credit in the short run. By 'in the short run' we mean without rewriting contracts; our data do not permit us to do anything to estimate the extent to which capital can be shifted through mutual agreement to modify the terms of new contracts. This short-run context does in fact seem to us to be the relevant one for analysis of balance of payments crises or the stability of a floating rate, although not for the different purpose of forming an estimate of the extent to which international capital flows effected through variations in commercial credit might be able to frustrate an attempt to conduct a monetary policy at variance with that in the rest of the world.

The question that we attempt to answer is the following. Suppose that the Bank of England had been committed to defending the then-existing exchange rate, and that the relatively tranquil situation that in fact prevailed had been suddenly disturbed in March 1975 by some event that caused a massive loss of confidence in sterling. How large, and how rapid, could the outflow of commercial capital have been?

Our estimates of the various sources from which an outflow could have come are shown in Table 6.3. These sources comprise all intra-MNC transactions which are settled by the use of flexible methods of settlement, on both export and import sides of the account, irrespective of the currency of invoice (since the MNC as a whole will benefit from an appropriate lead or lag even if the invoice currency is such that the local branch does not register larger profits). In contrast, trade between independent firms gives rise to the possibility of leading or lagging only where it is both settled using a flexible method of settlement *and* it is invoiced in a currency that gives the importer the benefit of any sterling devaluation: this means imports invoiced in foreign currency, and exports invoiced in sterling. Finally, it may be possible to lead imports being bought under cash against documents and acceptance of bills against documents, and not invoiced in sterling; but lagging is not possible for exports.

In each row of the table we show a 'central estimate', together with a 'high estimate' and a 'low estimate'. It is not, unfortunately, possible to interpret the latter as defining the limits of the range of plausible estimates, still less as defining the range within which the true value lies with 95% probability. What these outer estimates in fact represent are

Table 6.3. *Estimation of potential sterling outflow through leading and lagging* (March 1975)

Row	Average scope for leading/lagging (days)			Value of trade flow (£m./day)			Sum that could have been transferred (£m.)		
	High est. (1)	Central est. (2)	Low est. (3)	High est. (4)	Central est. (5)	Low est. (6)	High est. (7)	Central est. (8)	Low est. (9)
Leads									
1 Intra-MNC imports using flexible settlement methods	87	56	25	19.5	13.7	8.0	1,697	767	200
Other imports invoiced in foreign currency:									
2 flexible methods	62	37	12	7.1	5.7	4.7	440	211	56
3 c.a.d. & acceptance of bills	14	7	0	20.0	14.7	10.2	280	103	0
4 Arithmetic total	–	–	–	46.6	34.1	22.9	2,417	1,081	256
5 Adjusted total[a]	–	–	–	35.1	34.1	33.6	2,131	1,081	285
Lags									
6 Intra-MNC exports using flexible settlement methods	40	25	9	8.3	5.6	2.3	332	140	21
7 Other exports sold on flexible terms and invoiced in sterling	20	10	0	16.6	10.7	6.8	332	107	0
8 Arithmetic total	–	–	–	24.9	16.3	9.1	664	247	21
9 Adjusted total[a]	–	–	–	22.7	16.3	15.1	468	247	21
Leads and lags									
10 Total (adjusted[a])	–	–	–	–	–	–	2,599	1,328	306
Memorandum items									
Imports					65.1				
Exports					53.0				

Note:
[a] To allow for conditional probabilities (see text for explanation)
Sources: Tables 4.1, Section D, 4.2, Section D and 6.4

the values under the most extreme set of figures thrown up by our data. Clearly the true value could lie outside this range: if, for example, the true proportion of imports settled on open account were 50% rather than the 38% shown by our number of transactions measure or the 39% shown on a value basis, the sum that could have been transferred in row (2) might be more than £440 millions. Since the estimates in the final three columns all involve combining a number of estimates drawn from, or at least in the light of, our data, it might seem unlikely that all (or almost all) the true coefficients will lie to the same side of *both* of our estimates. To that extent one can say that the true value is likely to lie within the range shown by the high and low estimates, and that these give some feel for the probable degree of error. The high and low estimates do at least indicate that we are in the business of estimating orders of magnitude rather than figures that are meaningful down to the last million pounds.

We discuss first how the figures in the central three columns were constructed. Consider row (1). Table 4.2, Section D shows that 40% of the imports in our sample by value, and 17% by number of transactions, represented intra-MNC transactions. Since value is the relevant concept here but we believe the data by number of transactions to be more reliable, we split the difference to get an estimate that 28% of total imports were intra-MNC. The 40% figure is used to derive the high estimate shown in column (4), and the 17% to get the low estimate in column (6). Table 5.2 shows that 75% of our import sample of intra-MNC transactions by value, and 72% by number of transactions, were settled by a 'flexible' method of settlement. These figures are so close that it matters little which is taken, but in fact we used 75% as the central estimate to make some modest allowance for the possibility that intra-MNC transactions settled in nominally-inflexible ways may in fact contain a limited element of flexibility. Taking total imports of £1,953 millions per month (the average for the first half of 1975) and dividing by 30, the number of days in a month (since periods of credit include weekends), one gets the estimate of £13.7 millions per day shown in row (1), column (5), of Table 6.3. The corresponding high and low estimates were constructed by combining the 40% and 75%, and the 17% and 72%, coefficients respectively, with the same trade flow.

It would be tedious to repeat in similar detail the sources of the other entries in columns (4) to (6). The principles involved were the same: that is, the central estimate generally used the means of our results by value and by number of transactions in order to estimate the proportions of trade that fell in the various categories, while the high and low estimates always combined all the highest and all the lowest results, respectively. The one occasion when the central estimate was not taken as the mean of the results by value and by number of transactions was in selecting a figure for the proportion of intra-MNC exports settled using flexible methods, where a figure of 70% (rather than the mean of 63%) was used on the argument that the result by value of 50% was so far below all the three other estimates of intra-MNC settlement practices that it was probably distorted by the skewness problem to which we have already referred on many occasions.

The estimates shown in column (5) imply that our best estimate is that just over one half of import trade and one third of export trade is open to (short-run) leading and lagging respectively. If one similarly adds up the results in rows (1) to (3) in columns (4) and (6), one would conclude that between 17% and 72% of imports were exposed to leading. In fact, however, it is inconsistent to add up all the high or all the low estimates. For example, if 40% of imports were intra-MNC, as is assumed in forming the high estimate in row (1), then it is not possible for 83% to be transactions between independent firms, as is assumed in constructing the high estimates in rows (2) and (3). In other words the figures in the various rows are not independent, and this should be allowed for in summing the several entries to get the total. An appropriate adjustment to allow for conditional probabilities has therefore been made, and the results are shown in the 'adjusted totals' in rows (5), (9) and (10). It happens that the variation of the adjusted total in the high and low estimates around the central estimate is trivial on the import side (in relation to the value of the trade flow, though not in the sum that could have been transferred). This is just an accident, which results from the fact that the various factors happen to cancel out: it does not mean that the true value certainly lies between £33.6 and £35.1 millions per day, since as already pointed out the high and low estimates do not allow for the possibility that because of sampling error the true values of the coefficients lie outside the range defined by the two calculations made from our sample.

Estimates of the funds that could be shifted through leads and lags require estimates not merely of the size of the trade flows subject to leading and lagging, but also of the average number of days for which leading or lagging is possible. Our findings on periods of credit, already reported in Section 5.2, provide the basis for our estimate on this topic. The relevant findings are presented, using a slightly different classification to that in the previous chapter, in Table 6.4.

Our estimates presented in the first three columns of Table 6.3 were

Table 6.4. *Average terms of payment and credit terms* (days)

		Term of payment (concept *A*)	Credit term (concept *B*)
Imports			
Intra-MNC:	Group I	81	87
	Group II	74	74
Other:	Group I	57	62
	Group II	28	28
Exports			
Intra-MNC:	Group I	89	80
	Group II	119	128
Other:	Group I	52	62
	Group II	24	35

Note: Group I = flexible credit terms; Group II = inflexible credit terms (See Section 5.1)

based on the following reasoning. The high estimates in rows (1) and (2) were formed by reasoning that the maximum extent to which importers could lead would involve their paying all their outstanding bills on open account immediately. Since the credit term measures the interval between a payment being demanded and made, this provides the relevant concept, giving rise to the figures of 87 and 62 days drawn for Table 6.4. The low estimate in row (1) was found by reasoning that a conservative estimate to what MNCs could shift out was provided by supposing that they reduced the credit on their internal transactions to the same level of 62 days as that on trade between independent firms, implying a lead of 25 days. The central estimate was then placed midway between high and low estimates. The low estimate in row (2) was formed, rather arbitrarily, by placing it at half the corresponding figure for intra-MNC trade in row (1), and the central estimate was then again placed midway between high and low estimates. The entry for the low estimate in row (3) is put at zero because c.a.d. and acceptances do not necessarily allow leading. The maximum estimate is based on the supposition that leading of up to one half of the credit term is on average possible for transactions in this category.

On the export side, Table 6.4 shows that on average intra-MNC terms of payment in Group I were 9 days longer than credit terms, so that payments could certainly have been lagged a further 9 days. Indeed, since Group I transactions between independent firms had credit terms some 10 days longer than terms of payment, that is a very conservative minimum. Unfortunately there is no very persuasive basis on which to construct a high estimate: we put this figure, rather arbitrarily but hopefully not unreasonably, at 40 days. In view of the excess of credit term over term of payment for transactions between independent firms shown in Table 6.4, it is clearly appropriate to put the minimum additional lag at zero. The maximum is again a rather arbitrary estimate, of one half the lag possible on intra-MNC trade. Central estimates are again placed midway between high and low estimates.

The entries in columns (7) to (9) are calculated by multiplying entries in rows (1) to (3) by the corresponding entry in rows (4) to (6). These entries are then summed to get the 'arithmetic totals' shown in rows (4) and (8), but as already explained the high and low estimates yielded by this procedure give an exaggerated impression of the range of outcomes that is possible. The totals after allowing for non-independence between the rows are shown in rows (5) and (9), which are then summed in row (10) to give our estimate of the total volume of funds that could have flowed out through leading and lagging had there been an old-fashioned speculative crisis in March 1975.

Our central estimate of this potential capital outflow is £1,328 millions. Since over 80% of this total is accounted for by the leading of import payments, it seems quite appropriate to 'scale' this sum by the value of imports. Accordingly, we would say that our central estimate indicates that leads and lags could have amounted to something like two thirds of a month's imports. This is not of course a precise estimate: on the contrary, our high estimate is about one and a third month's imports, and our low estimate as little as 15% of a month's imports. The most that one can reasonably conclude is, perhaps, that leads and lags probably amount to something under a month's supply of imports in typical circumstances.[2]

Two points about the composition of this total are worth noting. The first is that some 70% of it is accounted for by intra-MNC transactions. The reasons are (a) that most of these are settled in a way that admits flexibility, and (b) that the periods of credit that branches of MNCs typically allow one another are long. Accordingly, under normal circumstances any branch of an MNC has substantial debts owing to other branches, the payment of which can be accelerated if this appears opportune in the light of expected exchange-rate (or other) developments, the liquidity position of the branch permitting. This finding, of the predominant role of intra-MNC payments in leads and lags, provides some substantiation for the charge that the adjustable peg provided an unintended subsidy for the multinationals. (This is not, of course, the same as charging the multinationals with impropriety in accepting the subsidy; indeed, we would have charged them with inefficiency had we found evidence that they had not made arrangements to cash in on the subsidy that used to be so generously offered them by the Bank of England.)

The second point worth noting is that, as remarked above, over 80% of the total is accounted for by the leading of import payments. In fact even the residual 20% *overstates* the role of lagging of export payments in the sort of sudden exchange-market crisis that we are considering. The reason is that (as initially noted by Uggla, 1970, p. 74) there is an important asymmetry in the time dimension applying to leads on the one hand and to lags on the other. Apart from possible liquidity constraints, the whole of the sum of over £1 billion that we have estimated to be subject to leading could be shifted over the exchanges in a single day: the entire accumulated stock of bills outstanding could all be paid immediately. With export lagging, on the other hand, the most that can be done is to interrupt the payment of bills. The estimate in row (9), column (5) of Table 6.3 implies that this would have led to an outflow of capital of some £16 millions per day. Even in a three-day crisis, such as that of June 1972, lagging would thus contribute no more than 5% of the flow to be expected from leading. Accordingly, while we shall continue to use the phrase because it is so well-established, it is really something of a misnomer to speak of 'leads and lags'; what matter, certainly in the sort

Table 6.5. *Estimates of the stock of mobile capital in the UK, March* 1975

(£ *millions*)

Source of mobile capital	High estimate	Central estimate	Low estimate
Variations in commercial credit:			
leading of import payments	2,131	1,081	285
lagging of export payments	468	247	21
invisible trade	747	286	44
total leads and lags	3,346	1,614	350
Foreign holdings of sterling:			
private	2,519	1,269	19
official	4,862	3,616	2,370
Total mobile capital	10,727	6,499	2,739
Memorandum item			
Official reserves		2,458	

Sources: Top 4 rows – Table 6.3 and calculations described in text. Bottom rows – Bank of England *Quarterly Bulletin*, various issues, tables on 'Exchange Reserves in Sterling . . .' and 'Reserves and Related Items', and calculations described in text.

of billion-dollar per day crisis that characterised the adjustable peg in its later years, are leads and not lags.

Table 6.5 presents an attempt to place the estimates of Table 6.3 in perspective by comparing its results with estimates of the quantity of capital that is mobile for other reasons, and with the official reserves that were available to finance capital outflows. The results of Table 6.3 are presented in the first two rows. Furthermore, as Paul Einzig emphasised (1968, Chapter 9), there is scope for leading and lagging payments for invisible as well as visible trade, whereas our estimates relate only to the latter. Perhaps regrettably, we made no attempt to include invisible trade within our survey, so that the most we can do here is to guesstimate. Our central estimate assumes that on average invisible trade allows half as much scope for leading and lagging as does visible trade, and is therefore formed by taking the estimates for visible trade and multiplying them by (a) the ratio between invisible and visible trade in the first half of 1975, and (b) one half. Our high and low estimates were formed similarly, using coefficients of two thirds and one third respectively in place of one half.

The only way in which exchange controls allowed UK residents to export capital on a net basis without explicit exchange control permission was through variations in commercial credit. However, sterling was convertible to foreign holders, and it is therefore necessary to add estimates of the foreign holdings of sterling that would have been withdrawn in a crisis. Here our high estimates are simply reported gross holdings of liquid sterling liabilities to private foreigners and of exchange reserves held in sterling, respectively. Our low estimates are formed by subtracting from those gross holdings the minimum levels to which holdings fell over the period end-1974 to end-1977, on the ground that those minimum actual holdings provide maximum estimates of the minimum working balances that are not withdrawn even in the event of a severe loss of confidence in sterling. It should, however, be stressed that these are very much maximum estimates (of minimum working balances, and therefore minimum estimates of mobile capital), because of the fact that sterling was floating over the period in question; had the pound been pegged, as is being hypothesised in constructing these estimates, it is likely that the actual withdrawal of funds from London in the Autumn of 1976 would have been substantially greater than actually occurred. (In fact private sterling balances were not run down at that time, although they were of course already at a low level.) Finally our central estimates are an average of the high and low estimates.

The central estimates shown in Table 6.5 suggest that in March 1975 the stock of mobile capital in sterling was over twice as large as the official reserves, and even the low estimate shows mobile capital exceeding the reserves. This is of course quite consistent with sterling's stormy history over the subsequent two years. Second, they show that the major form of mobile capital was at that time foreign official holdings of sterling – it should be remembered that this was the end of the period when the oil exporters used a substantial part of their new surpluses to build up holdings of sterling. Third, the figures suggest that variations in commercial credit contributed no more than some 25% of the stock of mobile capital, and were by themselves lower than the official reserves (except on the high estimate).

We interpret the latter findings as indicating that leads and lags were rather less important as sources of capital mobility than they have traditionally been pictured. It may well be that this reflects a change in reality rather than that the earlier impressionistic accounts of the role of leads and lags were incorrect. For all that was written about the problem of the sterling balances during the 1950s and 1960s, the fact is that foreign official holdings of sterling were remarkably stable until after the sterling devaluation of 1967. It is therefore entirely possible that leads and lags were of dominant importance in speculative capital movements prior to the 1970s. But our figures do suggest that in March 1975 the sterling balances provided a substantially larger source of potential outflow than did leads and lags – a potential outflow which in fact materialised over the following 21 months. Furthermore, the reserve build-up which followed the return of confidence in sterling in 1977 was financed principally by a build up of foreign private holdings of sterling, so it seems likely that leads and lags remained no more than a subsidiary source of capital mobility, even before the abolition of UK exchange controls in October 1979.

6.3 Synthesis

In Section 6.1 we explored the implications of trade financing practices under the assumption of capital immobility. However, one consequence of certain trade financing practices is to contribute to capital mobility. In Section 6.2 we therefore sought to estimate the stock of capital that could be shifted in this way, and to compare it with other sources of mobile capital. In the present section we endeavour to synthesise the results of the last two sections in order to form a judgment of the impact of trade financing practices on the operation of the foreign exchange market. It is convenient to do this by again discussing in turn each of the five distinct exchange-rate regimes considered in Section 6.1.

6.3.1 *Free floating*

In Section 6.1.1 it was shown that, given the fact that most trade is invoiced in the exporter's currency, a freely-floating exchange rate would be dynamically unstable in the absence of capital mobility. In fact, as illustrated in Section 6.2, capital is not immobile. When a currency depreciates, the short-run impact is indeed to worsen the current account; nevertheless, sooner or later some agents with mobile capital at their disposal will decide that the rate has depreciated beyond its equilibrium and is unlikely to depreciate further, and will become prepared to back this judgment by buying the depreciated currency. It is these speculative capital movements that serve to stabilise a system of freely floating exchange rates.

The fact that capital mobility can confidently be expected to eliminate the instability that would exist in a system of free floating without capital mobility does not, however, by itself imply that the instability theorem can be dismissed as a curiosum. If speculators were prepared to back their judgment with sums of money that were substantial in relation to the current imbalances only after they were certain that the rate had substantially overshot its equilibrium level, a random change in the current account could have an important impact on the exchange rate. In such circumstances the exchange rate, though not unstable, would be *volatile*; and such volatility also has economic costs. If, on the other hand, capital mobility were very high and asset-holders had well-determined views of the equilibrium exchange rate, then the exchange rate would be determined exclusively by the conditions of asset-market equilibrium[3] and the instability theorem would indeed be a mere curiosum. (In this type of model the current account imbalance influences the exchange rate only indirectly, by altering the asset positions of different wealth owners or perhaps by influencing expectations. See in particular Kouri in Herin et al., 1977).

Which of the above two models is the more useful description of reality is an empirical question, not one that can be unambiguously resolved on theoretical grounds. Even in a world where the stock of mobile capital is high, it is conceivable that most portfolio positions are not kept under continuous active review, but are maintained constant except when some event – such as a change in an exchange rate beyond some threshold – 'rings a bell'.[4] In that event the fact that the exchange rate has to be such that the existing stocks of the various currencies are willingly held does not in fact imply what it has commonly been taken to imply: namely, that a short-run imbalance between flow demand and supply on current account cannot influence the exchange rate (except indirectly). Some asset-holder has to take a decision to modify his portfolio position in order to finance a flow imbalance, and it is an empirical and not a theoretical question as to whether he will be prepared to do so without a perceptible change in the exchange rate.

The figures assembled earlier in this chapter seem to be helpful in forming a judgment on this empirical issue. In the first half of 1975, total current account payments were running at some £134 millions per working day, and total current account receipts at some £122 millions per working day (allowing 20 working days per month). There was thus an *average* difference between payments and receipts of £12 millions per day to be financed by capital inflow, and it can scarcely be doubted that this figure fluctuated greatly from one day to the next. In contrast, the invoice effect (the maximum J-curve effect) calculated in Section 6.1.2 from a 10% depreciation was something under £3 millions per working day. In other words, invoicing practices add only modestly to the imbalances which in any event have to be, and are, financed by the market. In further contrast, the central estimate of the stock of mobile capital in Table 6.5 was £6.5 *billions.* Variations in commercial credit alone could have financed the J-curve (from a 10% depreciation) for over two years at its maximum level (which certainly does not persist for anything like two years). Admittedly it is possible that speculators' expectations may be influenced by the published figures for the value of the trade balance. To the extent that they are so influenced and fail to make an appropriate allowance for the J-curve effect, its importance will be larger than indicated above. These figures, therefore, do not *prove* that the asset-market theory is correct and the instability theorem a curiosum, but they suggest that conclusion quite strongly.

It is worth noting as a curiosity that it is possible for the forward market to stabilise a market that would otherwise be dynamically unstable as a result of invoicing practices, and without requiring anyone to take an open position in foreign exchange. Suppose that there were a certain group of traders who not only cover their transactions forward, but who also decide whether or not to sign a contract according to the forward rate currently prevailing. Suppose also that the spot rate were declining and that there was no group prepared to stem this decline by taking an open position. If the decline in the spot rate were not accompanied by a decline in the forward rate, interest arbitrageurs would buy pounds spot and sell them forward. Their attempt to do this would in fact depress the forward rate, which would, by the above hypothesis, cause an increase in export contracts, and/or a diminution in import contracts, signed and covered forward. If trade responses were sufficiently sensitive to variations in the forward rate, the net demand for forward pounds by forward-rate sensitive traders would increase as the forward rate fell, thus matching the supply being provided by the interest-arbitrageurs, who would in turn maintain the spot rate. It is therefore possible to envisage circumstances in which the foreign-exchange market would be stable even without speculation. However, we doubt whether there in fact exists a substantial body of traders whose collective demand for forward exchange is elastic on a day-to-day basis as is assumed in this argument, and hence we judge that the case considered previously is the important one.

6.3.2 *The adjustable peg*

The implications of trade financing practices under the adjustable peg can be summarised very simply: they are inconvenient to the authorities. First, the J-curve effect can add to the problems they have in sustaining confidence in a new exchange rate following a realignment. This is both because it adds to the deficit to be financed, and because it makes the trade figures look worse than they really are. The first effect is not inevitable, in the sense that what really matters in this context is the trade balance on a balance of payments basis, and this can improve promptly following a devaluation if the market finds the new rate credible so that the leads and lags previously built up are quickly reversed (as happened in 1969 following the realignment of both the French franc and the Deutsche Mark). And rational expectations suggest that the second effect should never occur. However, there are certain historical experiences (e.g. sterling in 1968 or 1976, the dollar in 1973 or 1978) which give at least some reason to doubt whether exchange markets always act rationally, either in the technical or the general meaning of the term. It seems probable that the J-curve contributed something to intensifying the confidence problem at such times.

Second, and probably more important, are the implications of capital mobility. With a floating rate, capital mobility from some source is essential to permit the market to operate at all, and it therefore seems natural to welcome the additional capital mobility that is a consequence of flexible payments terms. Under the adjustable peg, however, the central bank provides the speculation that is necessary to stabilise the foreign exchange market, so there is not the same need to look to stabilising speculation by the private sector. The authorities would no doubt find it agreeable if the private sector moved capital in when the current balance was in deficit and out when it was in surplus, and when confidence in the parity is strong there is indeed a tendency for this to occur.[5] But when the parity is suspect precisely the reverse happens: capital flows out as the current deficit increases and in as the current surplus increases, since the current balance is rightly regarded as an important indicator of whether a devaluation or a revaluation is to be expected. This is without question highly inconvenient to the authorities.

Whether it should also be regarded as socially disadvantageous depends essentially upon whether the rate the authorities are defending is a disequilibrium rate or not. But even when speculation performs the social function of forcing the authorities to abandon the defence of an inappropriate rate, the profits made by the speculators involve a real cost to the central bank, and thus ultimately to the residents, of the country concerned.[6] It is true that this is merely a redistribution of income, but one may doubt whether the direction of redistribution that occurs as a result of flexible terms for trade payments – principally toward MNCs, and secondarily toward British importers – is one that would be chosen deliberately by policy.

6.3.3 *The crawling peg*

Capital mobility is not essential to the operation of a crawling peg, since the central bank can provide the finance necessary to stabilise the market and to bridge any J-curve effect that may exist, but neither is it as embarrassing to the system as it is to the adjustable peg. The higher is the degree of capital mobility, the less is the scope for interest rates to diverge from the international norm adjusted for the rate of crawl. However, provided that monetary policy is based on the control of domestic credit expansion at a rate consistent with announced intentions regarding the future rate of crawl, one might expect capital flows to be stabilising.

6.3.4 *Fixed exchange rates*

Fixed exchange rates preclude monetary independence in the long run; the higher is the degree of capital mobility, the shorter is that 'long run'. So long as the commitment to maintain a fixed exchange rate remains credible, capital flows can be expected to be stabilising.

6.3.5 *Managed floating*

The implications of capital mobility again depend upon the policy of exchange-rate management pursued.

As noted in Section 6.1.5, a policy of 'leaning against the wind' could not stabilise an otherwise unstable market, so capital mobility would be essential, as with a free float. Leaning against the wind would, however, have an effect on the numbers. In effect, every pound thrown into the market to offset a current surplus or deficit by some private agent taking an open position would elicit a matching contribution from the central bank. In a market where the volume of speculative funds was small relative to the size of current account imbalances, this might be important. In view of the numbers cited in Section 6.3.1, however, this consideration would seem to have little force, at least in the British context.

It was also noted in Section 6.1.5 that a policy of pursuing a target rate could stabilise a market which would otherwise be unstable as a result of invoicing practices. However, the figures cited in Section 6.3.1 again suggest that this consideration is not of great practical import. The case for target rates or allied concepts (such as the reference rate proposal) has to stand or fall on their ability to focus exchange-rate expectations in a stabilising way, and/or to offset destabilising capital movements.

There is no obvious reason to doubt that the 'unannounced, adjustable-under-pressure peg' will generate the same sort of to-the-authorities destabilising capital movements as does the *de jure* adjustable peg.

6.4 Concluding remarks

It seems clear from the preceding discussion that trade financing practices have their most important impact on the foreign exchange market under the adjustable peg. One might therefore conclude that the principal implication of our analysis is that it should have been undertaken ten or fifteen years earlier. However, with the periodic propensity of the authorities to embrace the unannounced, adjustable-under-pressure peg, it would be premature to reject the analysis as irrelevant.

7
POLICY IMPLICATIONS

The principal objects of our study were to establish the facts about trade financing practices, to see whether those facts could be understood, and to examine their implications for the operation of the foreign exchange market. Those purposes have now been accomplished, and accordingly the present chapter is more a postscript than a climax. Nevertheless, analysis of the type we have undertaken does suggest policy implications, even though often far from conclusively, and it is therefore worth discussing what we think these to be.

We start by considering the implications for British business, proceed to the implications for British government policy, and conclude by examining the implications for organisation of the international monetary system.

7.1 British business

In Chapters 4 and 5 we tested a number of hypotheses derived from the assumption that firms are risk averse and select their trade financing practices rationally in the light of that fact. Confirmation of these hypotheses would tend to suggest that firms act rationally and, accordingly, that there are no simple implications for the improvement of policy.

Including IIA as a separate hypothesis and counting VII (a) and (b) separately, we tested in all ten hypotheses. Of these, six were decisively supported by the data that we gathered on the financing practices of British traders, two were consistent with the data but were not statistically supported, one was consistent on the import side but not on the export side, and one was decisively rejected. One of the unsupported hypotheses (IIA) had such a small sample size that no great significance can be attached to the result: all of the other hypotheses on invoicing practices were confirmed. Of the two hypotheses on forward cover, one was rejected and one was unsupported. And of the three on method of settlement, two were confirmed and one was confirmed on the import side but not on the export side. To what extent can these results be considered as providing an endorsement or a criticism of the efficiency of British business in its trade financing practices?

So far as invoicing practices are concerned, our results suggest that firms in general know what they are doing. It is perhaps worth mentioning that we conclude this in part *because of*, rather than despite, the prevalence of sterling invoicing of exports. Hypothesis I implies that this is not a practice that deserves to be censored, nor do we believe that foreign currency invoicing can necessarily be considered more 'sophisticated'. This is contrary to a certain amount of comment that has appeared from time to time, in the press and elsewhere, in which it has been argued more or less explicitly that foreign-currency invoicing is a simple and rather sure way to increase the profitability of exporting which is carelessly ignored by the majority of British exporters in their unwillingness to break with their traditional habit of sterling invoicing.[1] The logic underlying blanket endorsement of foreign-currency invoicing has not to our knowledge been set out explicitly, but presumably it goes:

1. the price that influences a potential foreign buyer is the price in terms of his own currency at the time he is deciding whether to purchase, irrespective of the currency in which the contract is to be denominated; while
2. the price of interest to the exporter is the sterling value of the contract when payment is received, which, for a given price in sense (1), will be higher if the contract is denominated in foreign currency and the pound then depreciates between the time the contract is signed and the time payment is received.

The problems in this argument are virtually self-evident when it is stated explicitly. First, foreign purchasers are not generally indifferent between a contract that obliges them to pay £1,000 and one that obliges them to pay $1,951 in six months time, just because the sterling–dollar rate is £1 = $1.951 on the day the contract is signed. Foreigners also form views about the likely future course of exchange rates, and if they expect the pound to depreciate they will find the sterling-invoiced contract more attractive as surely as the British exporter will find it less attractive. Second, the pound does not always depreciate. There has been a trend in this direction which is bound to reassert itself in due course unless British inflation falls to the average of our trading partners, but, as experience since the end of 1976 has demonstrated, this is not a trend that can be relied upon to prevail over the time period of the typical trade contract.[2]

To criticise the view that foreign-currency invoicing is some sort of panacea is not, of course, to endorse the view that sterling invoicing is necessarily optimal, let alone that it is a patriotic duty. The essential point is that any presumption that invoicing in the currency of one rather than the other of the two trading partners is better rests upon some form of asymmetry between the positions of the two. The microeconomic theory which led us to Hypothesis I is based upon two forms of asymmetry that one expects to be generally present as between traders of differentiated products in different convertible-currency countries: the fact that it is the exporter who incurs costs of production, generally largely in his own currency, gives him a risk-averting reason for preferring his own currency to be used for invoicing; and the fact that it is the importer who has some freedom as to when to remit payment, which gives him some offset to the risk of being invoiced in a foreign currency that would not be available to an exporter. However, intuition does not suggest that these asymmetries are so powerful that they can never be outweighed by other asymmetries acting in the opposite direction. If, for example, a British exporter expects sterling to depreciate more (or appreciate less) than does his foreign trading partner, there may be scope for both to prefer a contract denominated in foreign currency. Or again it may be that, whether because they are accustomed to buying from domestic suppliers, or because the predominant competitors are from inconvertible-currency countries (recollect Hypothesis IV), or because their domestic currency is at the top of the hierarchy of currencies, some foreign purchasers are not experienced in dealing in foreign currency and consequently over-estimate the risks involved. There is no *a priori* reason why the net result of the various asymmetries that may be involved should not on occasion be to tip the balance of advantage in favour of foreign-currency invoicing, and our interviews with firms (Chapter 3 pp. 50–55) certainly suggest that this did indeed happen.

Consider next the question of method of settlement. Here Hypotheses VII(b) and VIII were confirmed, as was VII(a) in relation to imports. It may also be remarked that the interviews did not suggest that firms had any particular doubts or difficulties in this area. It was therefore a surprise to find that Hypothesis VII(a) was not satisfied by the export data. Nevertheless, there does not seem any obvious way of explaining away this result. We therefore suggest that those firms that allow flexible methods of settlement on foreign-currency invoiced exports should review their policy on this matter.

In regard to periods of credit and their variation we have a good deal less reliable information on which to draw; first, because we did not succeed in formalising any hypotheses to test in this area, and, second, because major progress probably requires a time-series analysis to study differences in behaviour in reaction to changes in conditions, rather than the cross-section analysis of a particular time that we undertook. Almost all we are able to say is that those firms interviewed were, in general, able to give a convincing rationale for most of their actions in this area. Perhaps one should add the qualification that all except one of the firms we interviewed denied making regular attempts to profit through leading and lagging, which we tend to regard as a practice that is desirable both from the standpoint of the individual firm and, under a floating exchange rate, of the economy – at least for those firms with sufficient knowledge to be able to expect to profit from adoption of this policy. However, we are not inclined to take these denials very seriously: first, because the major profit opportunities tend to arise not from 'regular' leading and lagging but from the occasional adoption of these practices at opportune moments; and, second, because what one is told on a subject as touchy as 'speculation' is likely to be at least in part what one's respondents think one will regard it as proper to hear. We therefore leave it an open question as to whether there are significant unexploited opportunities in this field.

There remains the question of the use made of the forward market. As has already been noted in previous chapters, the occasional questionnaire and a number of the interviews with firms suggested rather strongly that there is a good deal of ignorance about the forward market. Not only did some firms declare that they never covered because they did not understand the forward market, but others revealed that they adopted a policy of blanket coverage of all transactions. Our failure to find greater forward covering of larger transactions also supports the interpretation that use of the forward market is frequently not decided by rational calculation. We are therefore tempted to interpret our failure to find statistical confirmation of Hypotheses V and VI as a result of irrational policies on the part of British business. However, one has to ask whether this can explain the fact that Hypothesis V was not merely not confirmed but was refuted: i.e. that tradables II were significantly more likely to be covered forward than tradables I. If tradables II really do not need forward cover because price risk offsets exchange risk, why should so many importers of tradables II go to the extra trouble of using the forward market? Perhaps after all price risk does not always offset exchange risk for importers of tradables II, e.g. because the primary commodities are being imported by merchants who are making contracts to re-sell at a fixed sterling price at the same time as they are buying the imports. However, unless this type of factor, coupled with the narrow profit margins usual in wholesale trade, is so common as to more than outweigh the offsetting of price and exchange risks, one would still have to conclude either that importers of tradables I under-utilise the forward market or that importers of tradables II over-utilise it. Both the general supposition that errors of omission are more common than errors of commission and the evidence of ignorance of the forward market that we found in interviews combine to suggest the first explanation as the more probable.

We therefore conclude that there is a strong presumption that traders in tradables I were failing to take full advantage of the forward market at the time that our survey was exploring. The subsequent interviews suggested that use of the forward market was increasing, but that a good deal of ignorance remained. This picture is perhaps not altogether surprising in view of the generally limited benefits from use of the forward market under the pegged-rate system that persisted until 1971–72. (Benefits could be important on occasion when the Bank of England was supporting the forward rate.) Adaptations to the advent of floating do seem to be occurring and presumably cannot be completed overnight, especially to the extent that they require the employment of additional highly-trained personnel. Nevertheless, it is our impression that there is still a long way to go in this regard and ample opportunities to accelerate progress.

Perhaps we should add that we are not urging a policy of blanket use of the forward market, any more than we would advocate the adoption of a fixed rule in regard to choice of invoice currency, method of settlement, length of credit period, or date of payment. Our discussion should have made it clear that we do not believe there are mechanical rules that should be applied in any of these areas. There are, rather, some general principles that can be helpful in determining normal policy, and a host of particular factors that may make it worth while departing from normal policy – factors ranging from the size of the transaction, to the attitude of the trading partner toward exchange risk, to expectations about future exchange rates. Companies which command the necessary expertise can hope to benefit by exhibiting flexibility in modifying policy appropriately to meet particular circumstances. In many cases, however, the potential benefits involve accepting some additional risks, and improved performance would be conditional on expert and rational appraisal of where the possible extra profits are worth the cost in terms of heightened risk exposure. To return to the example of the forward market, almost any trader with foreign currency invoices who cannot match and does not benefit from automatic and complete offsetting of exchange risk by price risk can hope to benefit by taking forward cover on occasion. However, the benefit of forward covering depends on at least (a) the size of the transaction – because of wider buy/sell spreads in the forward market, the case is weaker for small transactions; (b) differences between the forward rate and the expected future spot rate; (c) the accuracy with which the date that payment is due to be made or received can be forecast; and (d) the attitude of the company toward accepting risk – which should be a function, among other things, of its liquidity position. Optimising – or even satisficing – in the light of a range of factors like this, some of which (such as forecasting expected future spot rates) themselves require the input of a good deal of knowledge and judgment, is the job of an expert.

In the hope of gaining some insight as to whether companies commanded such expertise and whether it had any systematic influence on their policies, we included a question on our questionnaire asking whether the respondent company had a specialist department dealing in foreign exchange. The results are reported in an Appendix to this chapter but, for reasons indicated there, we do not feel they shed much light on the issue. We are therefore left with the general judgment that, while the majority of firms appear well-informed on issues relating to the choice of currency used for invoicing, there may be scope for more active policies regarding variations in the period of credit and there is almost certainly a need for more informed policies relating to forward covering and for a more critical attitude toward allowing flexible methods of settlement on foreign-currency invoiced exports.

7.2 British government policy

The British Government had two instruments through which it can and does attempt to influence trade financing practices: the policies of the Export Credits Guarantee Department (ECGD), and exchange controls. We therefore start the present section by describing the work of the ECGD, and move on to a critical discussion of some of its policies. There follows a parallel evaluation of the relevant exchange control regulations. In addition, it is proper to ask whether trade financing practices have implications for policy in other areas. We believe that the principal instance of this arises in regard to the choice of an exchange-rate regime. We therefore take up this topic briefly at the end of the section.

7.2.1 *The Export Credits Guarantee Department* (*ECGD*)

ECGD is responsible to the Secretary of State for Trade. It endeavours to promote British exports, in two principal ways; firstly through the provision of credit insurance, and secondly by giving guarantees to banks to enable exporters to raise export finance at favourable rates of interest. Its operations are quite extensive: it has over 12,000 clients, and in 1978 covered about £12 billions of exports.

Insurance ECGD provides insurance coverage against the possibility that a UK exporter who has made a sale on credit, or a bank that has extended credit to a foreign buyer to permit the purchase of British goods, will not be paid. The former is known as 'supplier credit' and the latter as 'buyer credit'.

Two types of insurance policy are operated by ECGD. The first applies to regularly-repeated trade, involving more or less standard goods. In this case ECGD will not grant coverage for a single transaction, but requires that the bulk of an exporter's transactions for the entire year be covered. Transactions which can be covered or not, at the exporter's option, include those sold on terms such as confirmed letters of credit, and those sold to British merchants abroad. Lower premiums are charged to those exporters who cover all their export trade, on the ground that this provides ECGD with a spread of risks.

For projects of a non-repetitive nature, and large capital goods transactions, contracts are negotiated individually for each transaction. There is no requirement that all such business be covered, which of course means that an exporter may choose to cover only his worst risks. The premiums are, naturally, higher than for comprehensive coverage.

It is in general regarded as confidential when a supplier takes credit insurance from ECGD. The reason is to reduce risk of default. This rule is not, however, absolute; should a case be made that disclosure of the availability of credit insurance will help get the contract, then disclosure can be permitted.

For raw materials, semi-manufactures, and consumer goods, ECGD will cover credit of up to six months, which was the maximum credit period normally allowed by exchange control. With regard to other goods, credit insurance is readily available for periods of between two and five years if the goods are normally sold on such credit. Insurance of over five years may be given for very large projects, and may also be allowed where a foreign competitor is being assisted by his government. This latter exception raises the possibility of an export credit terms war, but efforts are made to avoid such an outcome. The Berne Union, of which ECGD was a founder member, exists in large part to that end. The Union, founded in 1934, currently has 35 members, including some private organisations, from 26 countries. It has no formal powers to prevent lengthening of government-aided credit terms, but relies on informal contacts to exercise moral suasion. In addition, the Organisation for Economic Cooperation and Development (OECD) has in recent years instituted a minimum rate of interest to be charged by its members on export credits. This common minimum interest rate is the same for all currencies; for contracts financed in foreign currencies the minimum always applies.

To reduce transaction costs, including particularly waiting time, a UK exporter of goods available for coverage under the comprehensive scheme can cover his expected year's exports in advance, subject only to limits on the amount of commitment with any one buyer. These limits, however, are low.

For orders from new buyers with up to £250 outstanding the exporter will normally be full credit insured so long as he has no adverse information on the buyer. Exporters can extend credit to a buyer with up to £5,000 outstanding on the basis of one satisfactory report from a bank or credit information agency. On the other hand, the range of risk covered is wide. It is as follows:

(i) insolvency of the buyer;
(ii) the buyer's failure to pay within six months of due date for goods which he has accepted;
(iii) the buyer's failure to take up goods which have been despatched to him (where not caused or excused by the policyholder's actions, and where ECGD decides that the institution or continuation of legal proceedings against the buyer would serve no useful purpose);
(iv) a general moratorium on external debt decreed by the government of the buyer's country or of a third country through which payment must be made;
(v) any other action by the government of the buyer's country which prevents performance of the contract in whole or in part;
(vi) political events, economic difficulties, legislative or administrative measures arising outside the UK which prevent or delay the transfer of payments or deposits made in respect of the contract;
(vii) war and certain other events preventing performance of the contract provided that the event is not one normally insured with commercial insurers;
(viii) legal discharge of a debt (not being legal discharge under the proper law of contract) in a foreign currency which results in a short-fall at the date of transfer.
(ix) cancellation or non-renewal of a UK export licence or the prohibition or restriction on export of goods from the UK by law (this risk is covered only where the pre-credit risk section of the guarantee applies).

The percentage of cover provided depends on which risk produces default; the percentage is 90% or 95%, except for (iii), where the exporter bears a first loss of 20% and ECGD pays 90% of the balance.

It can thus be seen that ECGD provides insurance coverage for credit of up to five years as a standard part of its business. It can also provide coverage, on a one-off basis, for transactions in capital goods (and for certain other specific types of contract, such as overseas construction projects) where credit of longer than five years is involved. Its coverage extends over all the lengths of periods of credit (by any definition) that we found.

Credit Except for credits of over five years maturity, export credits are provided by the banking system, either to the exporter or to the buyer. Both supplier credits and buyer credits are made at a 'preferential' (i.e. subsidised) interest rate, of 5/8 per cent over base rate. Credits of over two years maturity are made at a fixed rate of interest, with ECGD paying the banks the difference when market rates of interest are higher than the fixed rate (and collecting a refund from the banks if market rates fall below the fixed rate). Sterling credits of over five years maturity are refinanceable by ECGD.

Buyer credits, where the supplier receives payment from a bank and the buyer then repays the bank, have some advantages for the exporter. (These credits are available for capital goods contracts worth £1 million or more.) In particular, they are attractive to firms that are lightly capitalised in relation to turnover. ECGD's only contractual arrangement with the exporter is the premium agreement, whereby the exporter agrees to pay the premium on the loan that finances his contract.

Foreign currency invoicing ECGD credit insurance has for some time been available where exporters invoice in foreign currencies. Some additional cover was introduced in October 1976 when ECGD agreed to the payment of claims at the rate of exchange prevailing at time of loss rather than at time cover began.

The foreign currency financing scheme applies to capital goods exports usually supported under the buyer credit system, though there is a scheme for foreign currency specific bank guarantees for supplier credit contracts. The rules for foreign currency financing are:

1. ECGD seeks to underwrite large projects in foreign currency.
2. For contracts with a loan value of up to £5 million. ECGD generally expects to see non-sterling finance, but will not insist where the exporter or his financial adviser consider there is an advantage in using sterling.
3. For exports to EEC countries with credit terms of not more than five years, there is a similar option irrespective of the loan value. These contracts are not eligible for interest make-up support.
4. The interest rate on foreign currency financed contracts is set at the minimum established under the international guidelines.
5. All banks authorised under the Exchange Control Act 1947 and registered as companies in the UK are eligible to arrange these credits provided that when a managing bank is substantially owned by a non-UK registered company it shall not extend participation in the credit to other banks in the same group unless such other banks are themselves eligible to arrange financing under the scheme.

No doubt this change in policy has played some part in the recent move to foreign-currency invoicing of British exports revealed by the latest Department of Trade survey quoted in Table 2.1.

Several reasons for this change in policy have been given, not all of them convincing. First, it has been stated that 'when inflation in the UK is at a higher rate than in other industrial countries, there can be financial advantages in having debts [owed to one] in foreign currency'

(ECGD, 1977, p. 35). This takes us back to our discussion in Section 7.1 (p. 125), where it was implied that the response to this type of assertion is: but would the debts be the same size to begin with if they were expected to end up different? Second, it is argued that foreign-currency invoiced export credits promote a capital inflow. This is because the finance for such a credit can be, and usually is raised in the Euro market. At a time when there is a need for the country to borrow more, it makes good sense to encourage such borrowing; but as a regular policy to be applied even when the authorities are embarrassed at sterling's strength, it is absurd. Third, it is argued that such credits do not require ECGD refinancing, and thus keep down the public sector borrowing requirement. However, the reason they do not require ECGD refinancing is that the real interest rates are higher. It would be perfectly possible, and almost certainly desirable, to raise the rate of interest on sterling export credits to a level that would dispense with the need for ECGD refinancing (as has in fact already been done to some extent); it is not necessary to force foreign-currency invoicing on exporters to achieve this objective.

One reason that might be given for the switch in policy is that foreign-currency invoicing eases the task of macroeconomic management by eliminating the J-curve and reducing the incentives to lead and lag so as to take advantage of expected exchange-rate changes. This argument merits several comments. First, elimination of the J-curve would also be furthered by sterling invoicing of imports, and policy should therefore certainly not be one of hostility to sterling invoicing of trade in general. Admittedly there may not be much that can be done to encourage sterling invoicing of imports, but it would be unambiguously foolish to discourage such invoicing. Second, the analysis of Chapter 6 led us to conclude that the exchange-market implications of trade financing practices are not of great consequence, except perhaps under the adjustable peg (*de jure* or *de facto*). Indeed, under a floating-rate system capital mobility is in general a benefit rather than an embarrassment, and accordingly it would seem perverse to reduce the incentive to lead and lag by divorcing the benefit from the correct anticipation of exchange-rate changes from the decision as to when to remit payment. Third, even when capital mobility is an embarrassment (i.e. under the adjustable peg), foreign-currency invoicing cannot be expected to do that much to reduce it, in as much as the major source of capital mobility through leads and lags is found in intra-MNC transactions (Table 6.3), and in this case the incentive to lead or lag is independent of the currency of invoice. We therefore conclude that this argument is limited in applicability to the invoicing of *exports* under the *adjustable peg*, and that even then its quantitative importance is open to doubt. On the other hand, we have outlined in this book the microeconomic rationale for exporters to prefer invoicing in their own currency, and it can be argued that one of the

2. the inflation is perfectly anticipated;
3. purchasing power parity prevails throughout;
4. the real rate of interest is independent of the rate of inflation;
5. the time lags between order, delivery and payment are fixed.

The proof of the preceding proposition is as follows. Let

P_j = price level at time t_j
C_j = cost of production in prices prevailing at time t_j
i = nominal rate of interest
p = rate of inflation
$z = i - p$ = real rate of interest
f = rate of inflation in purchaser's country
r_j = exchange rate between purchaser's country and sterling at time t_j
X = contract price in sterling
ρ = importer's real discount rate
t_0 = date order is placed
t_1 = date costs of production are incurred.
t_2 = date of delivery and payment.

Given a fixed time lag between order and payment (assumption 5) the seller would want to maximise the real value of his profit at date t_2, i.e.

$$\{X - C_1 \exp [i(t_2 - t_1)]\}/P_2$$

In order to insulate this real profitability from a constant, known, neutral rate of inflation p, all that the exporter need do is to increase the contract price X above the level $\hat{X}$ that he would have charged in the absence of inflation, in proportion to the inflation that will occur in the interval from t_0 to t_2. This is accomplished by setting $X = \hat{X} \exp [P(t_2 - t_0)]$, which makes his real profitability:

$$\{\hat{X}e^{\rho(t_2-t_0)} - C_0 e^{\rho(t_1-t_0)} e^{i(t_2-t_1)}\}/P_0 e^{\rho(t_2-t_0)} = (\hat{X} - C_0 e^{z(t_2-t_1)})/P_0$$

which is independent of p provided that z is (assumption 4). Furthermore, given assumption 3 (purchasing power parity, which implies $r_j = r_0 \exp [(f-p)(t_j - t_0)]$, the present value at t_0 of the cost to the importer is

$$Xr_2 e^{-(\rho+f)(t_2-t_0)} = \hat{X} r_0 e^{-\rho(t_2-t_0)}$$

which is also independent of the rate of inflation. Under those conditions, cost escalation cover provides a scarcely-veiled subsidy to the capital-goods exporting industries. It follows that any case for the provision of such cover must be based on one or more of these conditions not holding. We therefore proceed to examine the implications of relaxing each of these assumptions in turn.

Inflation never is perfectly neutral. There is, however, no reason for supposing that the inevitable non-neutralities will systematically raise the costs of the capital-goods producing industries more rapidly than the prices of capital goods. The expected return to the exporter should therefore be independent of the rate of inflation. However, if firms are risk averse (as normally assumed), they will be sensitive not merely to the expected return but also to its variance. Given that relative prices tend to vary more the higher is the rate of inflation (Parks, 1978, p. 79), the variance of the return will tend to be higher with a faster rate of inflation. This would tend to discourage the production of all capital goods (those destined for the home market as well as for export).

Consider second the effect of relaxing the assumption that inflation is perfectly anticipated. What is critical is whether a higher actual rate of inflation leads to a greater *variance* of expectations of future inflation. If it does, for which there is considerable evidence (Okun (1971), Vogel (1974), Logue and Willett (1976), Heller (1976), Jaffee and Kleiman (1977)) then the customary assumption of risk aversion again leads one to conclude that inflation introduces a bias against the production of (all) capital goods. The reason is that, to maintain the expected utility of the producer's profits constant, his contract price will have to increase more than proportionately to his central estimate of the inflation rate over the period of the contract. The risk premium required by a British producer would provide a competitive margin to a foreign competitor in a low-inflation country.

Consider third the effect of relaxing the assumption that the exchange rate continually adjusts to maintain purchasing power parity. This makes no difference to the exporter as long as he is invoicing in sterling, but – assuming that contracts cannot be covered in the forward market, which is reasonable with contract periods of the length sometimes found in the capital goods industries – it does increase the risk to the foreign purchaser. The question, however, is whether that risk will be greater in the presence of inflation than with price stability – i.e. are the (temporary and short-run, for PPP is surely a useful medium-run first approximation) deviations from purchasing power parity greater under inflationary conditions? The supposition that they are seems plausible, but we are aware of no evidence to invoke in support. It should be noticed that in this case the bias is specifically against the production of capital goods for export, and not, as in the first two cases, against the production of capital goods for the domestic market as well.

Fourth, consider the implication of relaxing the assumption that the real rate of interest is independent of the rate of inflation. There is in fact reason to expect the real rate of interest to be lower with a high rate of inflation (Mundell, 1971, Chapter 2), and there is also considerable evidence that the theoretically-expected result actually occurs. The effect of this is to *increase* the profitability of the contract to the exporter. Furthermore, his gain is not at the expense of the importer: on the contrary, the latter would experience a decline in the present value of his costs, if he were being granted buyer credit. Both exporter and importer may gain, at the expense of the bank that provides the export credit during the (typically lengthy) period between delivery being made and the purchaser paying. More accurately, both parties gain at the expense of the bank's depositors: in fact, both get a little bit of the inflation tax – which hardly provides a reason for giving them a subsidy as well.

Finally, consider the possibility that the time lags are not all constant. The important point here is that the delivery date may be variable. A delay in delivery will impose a greater loss in (real) profitability if the inflation rate is high than if it is low. There is of course some offset from the possibility of early delivery, but with risk aversion this offset will not be complete. This effect again applies to all production by the capital goods producing industries and not just that for export.

We conclude that there are indeed some reasons for expecting that high inflation will discourage the capital goods industries, although there is also one offsetting factor. All except one of these reasons apply to the production of capital goods for the domestic market as well as for export. Indeed, it can be argued that under certain circumstances it may be easier to avoid an increase in risk on capital goods being produced for export than on those being produced for the domestic market, because of the possibility of invoicing in a low-inflation foreign currency. If purchasing power parity holds fairly closely, this may make it possible to substantially eliminate the second and fifth sources of risk. It therefore seems safe to conclude that, if inflation does justify some special action to help the capital goods industries, that action should certainly *not* take the form of cost escalation cover on export contracts.

7.2.2 *Exchange control*

It is clear from the analysis of Chapter 6 that attitudes towards attempts to limit capital mobility through exchange controls may depend greatly on the exchange-rate regime in force. Under the adjustable peg (or its *de facto* variant, which we have termed the unannounced, adjustable-under-pressure peg), it is natural for the authorities to seek to suppress capital movements, including those that are effected through variations in commercial credits. To this end British exchange controls required that foreign currency earnings be converted immediately into sterling, that foreign exchange not be bought before it is needed to make a payment, that export credits be limited to six months except where specific permission had been sought from the Bank of England of ECGD, and that imports not be paid for in advance of their shipment to the UK (again except with specific permission).

If one is going to have exchange controls, these rules do not appear unreasonable, and they provoked few complaints in our interviews. However, the continued existence of such rules should not be taken for granted, especially now that the adjustable peg has been abandoned, in name and for the time being at least also in fact. Under a system of floating rates, as outlined in Chapter 6, capital mobility is essential to permit the market to function effectively, or indeed at all. It is true that the calculations made in that chapter indicated fairly conclusively that the degree of capital mobility now prevailing is sufficient to preclude the instability problems that could in principle arise in the absence of capital mobility, and one cannot therefore argue that liberalisation is essential to the satisfactory operation of the foreign exchange market under floating rates. Nevertheless, there would seem to be some presumption that more capital mobility is better than less, unless there is a specific reason for believing that a particular group is likely to speculate in a destabilising way.

We know of no such 'specific reason' that can be justified in the case of the traders who are in a position to export or import capital through variations in commercial credit. On the contrary, one might think that an inherently-limited stock of mobile capital that can be switched fast is more likely to play a stabilising role than is a large stock subject to slow adjustment, where extrapolative expectations can take hold and be self-fulfilling for a period of many months or possibly even years. It is sometimes said (and was said by some of our bank interviewees) that traders should stick to their own business and not get involved in speculation in the exchange markets. But it can equally well be argued that the very fact that traders are not involved directly in the exchange markets may make them a bulwark relatively immune to contamination by extrapolative expectations formation when the markets become feverish. We would not pretend that these arguments are conclusive, but our own sympathies are for liberalisation of the exchange control rules, including those governing access to the forward market; we therefore welcome the UK's abolition of exchange controls.

7.2.3 *The exchange rate regime*

It was argued in Chapter 6 that trade financing practices have their principal implications under the adjustable peg, where they are liable to be inconvenient to the authorities. Attempts to remove these inconveniences, by pressuring exporters into foreign-currency invoicing or by suppressing leads and lags, would almost inevitably impose microeconomic distortions.

There are of course other relevant factors that have to be taken into account as well in choosing an exchange rate regime. The fact that trade financing practices create difficulties for the adjustable peg that could be eliminated only by creating microeconomic distortions is one factor that should count against that system, including its *de facto* variant. But it would be beyond the scope of this study to presume to say more.

7.3 International monetary organisation

Our study seems to yield implications regarding the desirable shape of the international monetary system in two directions. The first is simply the international extension of the conclusion regarding the choice of exchange-rate regime that we have just drawn for Britain: namely, that trade financing practices provide a reason for avoiding the adjustable peg (known in IMF language as 'stable but adjustable par values'). It remains true that there are many other factors relevant to making a rational decision on this issue, but the potential for capital mobility through leads and lags undoubtedly contributed to the difficulties in sustaining the adjustable peg that caused the system to be abandoned in March 1973. It is to be hoped that any future reform efforts will pay more attention to the need to respect these facts of life than the Committee of Twenty did in 1972–74.[4]

The second direction in which it is possible to draw implications is in regard to the role of private 'international money'. By this we mean a monetary unit to serve the classic monetary functions of means of payment (between private parties in different countries) and unit of account (currency of invoice), which seems to be what has usually been embraced under the term 'vehicle currency'. (There are other functions of 'international money', at the official and inter-bank levels as well as the level of traders; for a taxonomy and a discussion of the extent to which different moneys can fulfil the different functions of money, see Cohen, 1971.) At one extreme, the so called 'vehicle-currency' hypothesis pictures most international transactions being settled by transfers of working balances maintained by traders in a single currency. At the other extreme, Grassman's symmetry hypothesis maintains that most international transactions are settled by importers drawing on their domestic bank accounts to buy the currency of the exporter in order to pay him a sum specified in his domestic currency. The second hypothesis tends to suggest that there need be no inherent difficulty in creating an international monetary system in which the various currencies are treated symmetrically, as was sought by the Committee of Twenty. In contrast, the vehicle-currency hypothesis suggests that a search for symmetry would be costly (Cooper, 1972), unless at least symmetry could be accomplished by developing an international asset (henceforth assumed to be the SDR) to fill the vehicle-currency role.

Our empirical results have tended to suggest that the truth lies somewhere between these two extreme visions of the system. In general we replicated the result found by Grassman for Sweden: that trade is predominantly invoiced in the currency of the exporter. However, the qualifications to this result are quite important. First, we found evidence of a role for vehicle currencies in the invoicing of primary commodities

(Hypothesis II). Second, we concluded that there is a distinct 'hierarchy of currencies' evident in the invoicing of tradables I (Section 4.1), with the currencies with the most extensive international role being used to an important extent to invoice those countries' imports as well as their exports. It may also be remarked that the existence of 'hold accounts' (Section 1.1) indicates that quite a number of firms find that they can reduce transactions costs by holding balances in a vehicle currency. Furthermore, although our study has not touched on the question, there seems little doubt that vehicle currencies play a dominant role in denominating international debts, both in the long-term international capital market and in the short-term (offshore bank) market.

We therefore conclude that, despite the similarity of our overall results with those of Grassman, there is something in the idea that transactions costs can be and are reduced by the use of a vehicle currency. The question which this raises for international monetary organisation is whether the vehicle-currency role can be better performed by a national currency, which would therefore inevitably have an asymmetrical position in the system (at least in some ways) in consequence, or by an international asset like the SDR (as urged, for example, by Chrystal, 1978).

One can envisage at least two benefits from the replacement of the dollar by the SDR in the vehicle-currency role.

1. In a world of floating exchange rates where the vehicle-currency country supplies only a small proportion of total world exports, appreciations and depreciations of that currency will inevitably occur, and will result in capricious variations in the purchasing power of exports denominated in the vehicle currency. This may be important both for exports that have an administered price set in terms of the vehicle currency (e.g. oil), and for those commodities whose price is determined by demand and supply on an international market in terms of the vehicle currency, and in which payment is delayed until significantly after a contract is signed. These capricious variations cannot be totally eliminated unless all currencies follow purchasing power parities all of the time, but for a country with a reasonably typical import composition they might be significantly reduced if the SDR, defined as at present as a basket of the principal currencies weighted by shares in world exports, were to take over the vehicle currency role.
2. International investors prefer to place their funds in strong currencies. International borrowers have to borrow in those currencies because it is only in those currencies that financial intermediaries have funds available to lend, but they borrow with a certain reluctance. The net result is to push up, or to sustain above its purchasing power parity,

the value of a currency acquiring a vehicle-currency role in respect to capital movements (the dollar in the 1960s, perhaps the Swiss franc in the 1970s). Sooner or later this leads to a current account deficit, pressures for depreciation, and then an exaggerated depreciation as investor confidence is shaken while borrowing is stimulated. There is an obvious parallel to the story of the reserve currency cycle as told by Triffin (1960). The solution may also be similar: the concentration of international borrowing and lending in terms of an international asset whose value is immune to the current account positions of individual countries.

Whether these two (and any other) benefits of replacing the dollar by the SDR in vehicle-currency uses by private parties would be worth the trouble of disrupting existing practices would seem to be an important topic that has not yet received the attention in the literature that it surely deserves. It is of course a fact that money enjoys economies of scale – that people want to hold the same vehicle currency that others are already holding, for a currency would hardly be much use as a vehicle currency if one were the only person holding it for that purpose. This means that to substitute the SDR for the dollar would almost certainly require the adoption of some form of rules or inducements to persuade people to switch to the SDR, at least during a transitional 'infant currency' period. One such rule would be to require international transactions to be invoiced in the SDR. The fact that most traders prefer to avoid invoicing in a third currency suggests that such a requirement would impose some cost in terms of inefficiency, although the fact that invoicing patterns vary so much depending on the position of a currency in the hierarchy perhaps suggests that this cost might be minimal. On that inconclusive note we leave this interesting topic.

7.4 Concluding remarks

We have now extracted such policy implications as seem to flow from our results. They are not dramatic, but that was to be expected in as much as the project was designed around the observation and understanding of a set of practices rather than around a particular policy problem. We nevertheless hope that such conclusions as we have drawn may provide a useful input into future analysis of policy options.

In seeking to understand British trade financing practices we chose to construct and test a number of formal hypotheses. It may interest readers to know that, while these hypotheses were changed in a number of ways while we were considering how they could be tested with the data yielded by our questionnaire, the hypotheses reached their final form *before* the data from the main survey were available. We deliberately avoided the equivalent of data mining: had we picked new hypotheses to fit the data and thrown out those that did not perform as expected, we could no doubt have achieved a more impressive-looking score than six supported hypotheses out of ten. Of course, we endeavoured to establish and to explain empirical regularities in our results even when we had not anticipated them *ex ante*; but these regularities recognised *ex post* were not formalised as hypotheses. They are a legitimate source of evidence on which we have indeed drawn in extracting implications in these last two chapters, but they have not been subjected to proper scientific testing, as we believe we can claim the hypotheses to have been.

Appendix to Chapter 7 – Specialist foreign exchange departments

Question C.1 on the questionnaire asked companies whether they had a specialist department (or group of staff) dealing in questions of foreign exchange. The responses, and some details of the association with the policies adopted, are shown in Table 7.1.

Section A shows that one third of the export transactions, covering one half of the value of exports, and a quarter of the import transactions which covered some 40% of the value of imports, were accounted for by firms that had such departments. The larger transactions were, therefore, more likely to involve a firm with such a department; presumably this is because, as Section B of the table shows, these departments tend to be concentrated in the larger firms, which also tend to be involved in the larger transactions.

Section C deals with differences in invoicing practices between firms with and without such a department. Differences were negligible on the import side (at least as measured by number of transactions), but firms with specialist departments were more prone to invoice exports in foreign currencies, especially the larger transactions. However, there is a possible problem of reverse causation that prevents one inferring that the better-informed firms made greater use of foreign-currency invoicing (although the data are of course consistent with that interpretation): namely, that a firm which finds it advantageous to invoice in foreign currencies presumably has a greater need for a specialist foreign exchange department. The same problem of interpretation arises with the finding that (except as measured by value on the import side) firms with specialist departments are more prone to cover forward (Section D). There is also, of course, a problem in knowing how good a measure of expertise is furnished by the existence of a specialist department.

Table 7.1. *Numbers of transactions, and policies, of firms with and without specialist foreign exchange departments*

	Exports		Imports	
	By firms with SDs	By firms without SDs	By firms with SDs	By firms without SDs
A *Number of transactions*				
Number of transactions	416	836	234	667
Percentage	33.2	66.8	26.0	74.0
Value of trade (£ thousands)	8,385	8,020	5,768	8,140
Percentage	51.1	48.9	41.5	58.5
B *Number of transactions by size of company turnover*				
Under £1 million	11	104	34	248
£1m. – £10m.	151	505	101	307
£10m. – £100m.	175	208	65	66
Over £100 millions	70	13	18	7
C *Percentage by currency of invoice*				
By number of transactions				
Seller's currency	81.7	87.3	62.4	64.0
Buyer's currency	14.4	9.8	29.9	27.6
Third currency	3.8	2.9	7.7	8.4
D *Percentage of foreign-currency invoiced transactions covered forward*				
By number of transactions	18.4	9.4	40.2	15.1
By value	19.0	4.7	36.5	36.1
E *Method of settlement* (percentage using open account)				
By number of transactions	42.5	46.8	47.0	43.8
By value	31.8	22.1	57.4	32.1

SDs = specialist foreign exchange departments
Source: Questionnaire survey

NOTES

Notes to introduction

1 This definition is narrower than that adopted by Paul Einzig (1968, p. 13), who also included changes in the timing of exports and imports, changes in the country or currency in which trade is financed, changes in the currency of invoice, and changes in forward cover, when any of these were induced by changes in views of the strength of currencies.

Notes to Chapter 1

1 Variations in the gap, or a constant-sized gap in the presence of growing world trade, provide an important part of the explanation as to why the world total of exports does not equal that of imports (f.o.b.) during any specific time period.

2 Actually, as may be inferred from subsequent discussion (pp. 10–12) of 'exchange risk' versus 'price risk', it is not true that invoicing or being invoiced in one's home currency is *necessarily* risk reducing. It is conceivable that a firm invoiced in its domestic currency might seek forward cover to reduce its net exposure to risk even though it had no foreign exchange exposure *per se*.

3 It should also be stated that there is a second difference in the way that we have *measured* concepts B and C: the former measured t_P as the date payment was *received* by the exporter, while the latter measured it as the date payment was *made* by the importer. In individual instances it appears that the time taken for the payment to be transmitted can be quite lengthy (due, for example, to poor banking facilities or exchange control problems), but we are reasonably confident that this factor makes little difference to the aggregate result, which is principally a reflection of disparities between the start of the credit term and delivery to the buyer.

4 This classification is not novel, although its application in this area is. The distinction is similar to that drawn by Hicks (1974) between 'fixprice goods' and 'flexprice goods'.

5 It should be noted that even for tradables I 'price risk' may to some extent offset 'exchange risk'. (See following paragraph for definitions.) This would occur if a devaluation of the importer's currency enabled him to raise his selling price and thus increase the domestic-currency value of his inventory. Where this is possible *all* (net) exchange risk can be eliminated by *partial* forward cover.

6 The nomenclature is due to Aliber (1976).

Notes to Chapter 2

1 Remember that this is how the United States and United Kingdom were referred to collectively in the 1960s.

2 In general only alternate years have been taken for display from Page's figures. Figures for Finland have been omitted entirely on grounds of non-comparability (a mixture of export and import figures and calculation of some currencies by residual). It appears likely, however, that the proportion of Finnish exports invoiced in domestic currency is substantially lower than for any other country shown.

3 'Buyer credits' involve the exporter receiving payment from a bank, which is subsequently reimbursed by the importer. 'Supplier credits' are those extended directly by the exporter. See Section 7.2 for further discussion.
4 It should perhaps be remarked that the enquiries omit the nationalised industries and oil.
5 However, other methods of settlement can provide some scope for flexibility, especially by leading (prepayment of imports), as noted in more detail in the next chapter.
6 Brittan (1977) discussed precisely this phenomenon, presenting Horsnail's calculation that in the year 1976, when sterling generally depreciated much more rapidly than it would have done if the forward discount had correctly anticipated the future spot rate, it may have resulted in an overstatement of imports of more than 1%.

Notes to Chapter 3

1 A detailed description of the various methods of settlement, together with an account of their origins and comments on their respective legal standings, can be found in Whiting (1973).
2 In some countries, however, the buyer can legally *demand* the documents upon acceptance, even though the exporter has ordered the documents to be given only upon payment.
3 The word 'fluctuating', with its implication of movement in both directions, is used deliberately, since use of the forward market cannot enable a firm to insulate itself against a *trend* in the spot rate.
4 One example is 'clean bills', which are bills not attached to any document of entitlement. They constitute a bill which the exporter draws on the buyer while sending the documents of entitlement direct to the buyer. This gives the seller no control over the documents, and hence demands as much trust between traders as does open account. One may conjecture that this method has been superseded by the greater simplicity of open account.
5 It might be remarked that the practices recommended tend to maximise not only the trader's security but also the bank's profit – both because of the generally wider buy/sell spread on the forward market as compared to the spot market, and because if a formal document is used in settlement the bank earns a commission by issuing it.

Notes to Chapter 5

1 Fuller definitions of the various methods of settlement can be found in Section 3.1.
2 The absence of 'free deliveries' from our sample presumably reflects the difference in the method by which our data were gathered rather than necessarily differences in behaviour as compared to Sweden. We asked firms to inform us about an 'invoice', which is a document that does not exist when no payment is due, whereas Grassman's data were based on transactions *registered with Customs.*
3 Cash against documents and acceptance of bills against documents are somewhat more flexible than the other methods of settlement in this category, in that they sometimes allow leading (though not lagging) of payments. However, in a binary classification it seems clear that they should be grouped with the inflexible rather than the flexible methods.
4 Unless, that is, he resorts to the extreme of accelerating or retarding sales of the goods.
5 It is, however, significant at the 5% level (for which the critical value of *chi*-square with one degree of freedom is 3.84).
6 Except in Section A, figures are given only on the basis of the number rather than the value of transactions. The value figures showed a number of erratic results that were biased by a few large transactions, and the results presented in Sections E of both tables suggest that size is not a systematic factor influencing periods of credit.
7 It should perhaps be remarked that the term of payment was defined, in the case of consignments, up to an ultimate credit limit, where such was specified, or to 180 days (the maximum permitted by exchange control regulations), whichever was the shorter.

Notes to Chapter 6

1 In fact it is of course the banks of the importers (or exporters) who deal in the market, and then only to the extent that they do not have mutually-offsetting credits and debits and sufficiently small remaining net positions to be accommodated by variations in their open positions in foreign exchange. However, this institutional detail makes no essential difference to the argument and is therefore suppressed.

2 It may be remarked that this relationship between potential capital outflow and the value of imports provides a possible rationale for the common but much-criticised practice of treating the reserves/imports ratio as a measure of reserve adequacy.

3 The asset-market view of exchange-rate determination was largely developed in the papers by Dornbusch, Kouri and Mussa in Herin, Lindbeck and Myhrman (1977).

4 See the suggestive discussion of this topic in Foley (1975).

5 See, for example, Kouri and Porter (1974).

6 An exception used to arise when the country to change its par value was the United States. On account of the reserve role of the dollar, the costs of successful speculation were largely borne by the central banks of the partner countries into which funds were moved.

Notes to Chapter 7

1 See, for example, Lawless (1977).

2 Any firms that were foolish enough to have followed the advice proffered in the article cited in the previous footnote must have paid a heavy price in the course of sterling's appreciation during 1977.

3 The classic example involves the manipulation of hire purchase terms. For example, the controls on cars were altered ten times during the 1960s, which is widely believed to have helped reduce the British motor industry to its present lamentable state.

4 This point has been argued before by one of the present authors (Williamson, 1977, Chapters 2 and 5).

Bibliography

R. Z. Aliber (1976), 'The Firm under Pegged and Floating Exchange Rates', *Scandinavian Journal of Economics*, 1976(2).

Bank of England (1976), *Bank of England Quarterly Bulletin*, June 1976.

Board of Trade (1968), *Board of Trade Journal*, 16 August 1968.

– (1969), *Board of Trade Journal*, 3 September 1969.

British Importers Confederation (1975), Directory of British Importers, Trade Research Publications, 1975.

S. Brittan (1977), 'Trade Figures May Be Wrong', *Financial Times*, 21 February 1977.

Central Statistical Office (1976), *Monthly Digest of Statistics*, July 1976.

K. Alec Chrystal (1978), International Money and the Future of the SDR. International Finance Section, Princeton University, Princeton, New Jersey, June 1978.

B. J. Cohen (1971), *The Future of Sterling as an International Currency*, Macmillan, London, 1971.

Committee on the Working of the Monetary System (Radcliffe Report) Cmnd 827, HMSO, London 1959.

R. N. Cooper (1972), 'Eurodollars, Reserve Dollars, and Asymmetries in the International Monetary System', *Journal of International Economics*.

Department of Trade (1971), *Trade and Industry*, 14 April 1971.

– (1975), *Trade and Industry*, 11 April 1975.

– (1977), *Trade and Industry*, 12 August 1977.

– (1978), *Trade and Industry*, 5 May 1978.

R. Dornbusch (1977), 'The Theory of Flexible Exchange Rate Regimes and Macroeconomic Policy' in J. Herin, A. Lindbeck, and J. Myhrman, eds., *Flexible Exchange Rates and Stabilization Policies*, Macmillan, London 1977.

Dun and Bradstreet (1976), *Guide to Key British Enterprises*, 1975/6 edition.

ECGD (1977), ECGD Services, London, 1977.

ECGD (1978), ECGD Services, London, 1978.

P. Einzig (1962), *A Dynamic Theory of Forward Exchange*, Macmillan, London, 1962.

–(1968), *Leads and Lags: The Main Cause of Devaluation*, Macmillan, London, 1968.

Extel Statistical Service, British Company Annual Cards.

– Unquoted British Companies Annual Cards.

N. Fieleke (1971), 'The Hedging of Commercial Transactions between US and Canadian Residents', *Canadian–US Financial Relationships*, Federal Reserve Bank of Boston, 1971.

D. Foley (1975), 'On Two Concepts of Asset Market Equilibrium', *Journal of Political Economy*, April 1975.

S. Grassman (1967), 'The Balance of Payments Residual', *Skandinaviska Banken Quarterly Review*, 1967(2).

– (1973a), *Exchange Reserves and the Financial Structure of Foreign Trade*, Saxon House, Farnborough, 1973.

– (1973b), 'A Fundamental Symmetry in International Payment Patterns', *Journal of International Economics*, May 1973.

– (1976), 'Currency Distribution and Forward Cover in Foreign Trade: Sweden Revisited, 1973', *Journal of International Economics*, May 1976.

B. Hansen (1961), *Foreign Trade Credits and Exchange Reserves*, North Holland, 1961.

B. Hansen & T. Nilsson (1960), 'Foreign Trade Credits', *Skandinaviska Banken Quarterly Review*, July 1960.

H. R. Heller (1976), 'International Reserves and World-Wide Inflation', IMF Staff Papers, March 1976.

J. Herin, A. Lindbeck, & J. Myhrman, eds. (1977), *Flexible Exchange Rates and Stabilization Policies*, Macmillan, London, 1977.

J. R. Hicks (1974), *The Crisis in Keynesian Economics*, Blackwell, Oxford, 1974.

D. Jaffee & E. Kleiman (1977), 'The Welfare Implications of Uneven Inflation' in E. Lundberg, ed., *Inflation Theory and Anti-Inflation Policy*, Boulder, Col., 1977.

S. Katz (1953), 'Leads and Lags in Sterling Payments', *Review of Economics and Statistics*, February 1953.

L. J. Kazmier (1973), *Statistical Analysis for Business and Economics*, McGraw Hill, New York, 1973.

M. Kemp (1964), *The Pure Theory of International Trade*, Prentice-Hall, New Jersey, 1964.

J. M. Keynes (1923), *A Tract on Monetary Reform*, Macmillan, London, 1923.

P. J. K. Kouri & M. G. Porter (1974), 'International Capital Flows and Portfolio Equilibrium', *Journal of Political Economy*, May/June 1974.

P. J. K. Kouri (1977), 'The Exchange Rate and the Balance of Payments in the Short Run and in the Long Run: A Monetary Approach', in J. Herin, A. Lindbeck, & J. Myhrman, eds., *Flexible Exchange Rates and Stabilization Policies*, Macmillan, London, 1977.

J. Lawless (1977), 'How to stay on top of the Ups and Downs', *Sunday Times*, 6 February 1977.

D. E. Logue & T. D. Willett (1976), 'A Note on the Relation between the Rate and Variability of Inflation', *Economica*, May 1976.

E. Lundberg, ed. (1977), *Inflation Theory and Anti-Inflation Policy*, Boulder, Col., 1977.

S. P. Magee (1974), 'US Import Prices in the Currency-Contract Period', Brookings Papers on Economic Activity, 1974(1).

R. J. McKinnon (1969), 'Private and Official International Money: the Case for the Dollar', Princeton Essays in International Finance, No. 74, 1969.

– (1979), *Money in International Exchange: The Convertible Currency System*, Oxford University Press, New York, 1979.

M. Mussa (1977), 'The Exchange Rate, the Balance of Payments and Monetary and Fiscal Policy under a Regime of Controlled Floating', in J. Herin, A. Lindbeck, & J. Myhrman, eds., *Flexible Exchange Rates and Stabilization Policies*, Macmillan, London, 1977.

R. A. Mundell (1971), *Monetary Theory*, Goodyear Publishing Co., Pacific Palisades, California, 1971.

A. Okun (1971), 'The Mirage of Steady Inflation', Brookings Papers on Economic Activity, 1971(2).

S. A. B. Page (1977), 'Currency of Invoicing in Merchandise Trade', *National Institute Economic Review*, August 1977.

R. W. Parks (1978), 'Inflation and Relative Price Variability', *Journal of Political Economy*, February 1978.

R. Triffin (1960), *Gold and the Dollar Crisis*, Yale University Press, New Haven, 1960.

C. Uggla (1970), 'Commercial Credits and Corporate Covering of Foreign Exchange Positions', *Skandinaviska Banken Quarterly Review*, September 1970.

M. Van Nieuwkerk (1979), 'Exchange Risks in the Netherlands International Trade', *Journal of International Economics*, February 1979.

R. C. Vogel (1974), 'The Dynamics of Inflation in Latin America, 1950–69', *American Economic Review*, March 1974.

D. P. Whiting (1973), *Finance of Foreign Trade and Foreign Exchange*, MacDonald & Evans, London, 1973.

J. Williamson (1965), *The Crawling Peg*. Princeton Essays in International Finance, No. 50, 1965.

– (1977), *The Failure of World Monetary Reform*, 1971–74, Nelson, London, 1977.

G. E. Wood & S. Carse (1976), 'Financing Practices in British Foreign Trade', *The Banker*, September 1976.

INDEX